RUN YOUR BUSINESS, DON'T LET IT RUN YOU

RUN YOUR BUSINESS, DON'T LET IT RUN YOU

LEARNING AND LIVING PROFESSIONAL MANAGEMENT

CLAY MATHILE

Berrett–Koehler Publishers, Inc.
San Francisco
a BK Business book

Berrett-Koehler Publishers, Inc.
235 Montgomery Street, Suite 650
San Francisco, CA 94104-2916
Tel: (415) 288-0260   Fax: (415) 362-2512   www.bkconnection.com

Ordering Information
Quantity sales. Special discounts are available on quantity purchases by corporations, associations, and others. For details, contact the "Special Sales Department" at the Berrett-Koehler address above.
Individual sales. Berrett-Koehler publications are available through most bookstores. They can also be ordered directly from Berrett-Koehler: Tel: (800) 929-2929; Fax: (802) 864-7626; www.bkconnection.com
Orders for college textbook/course adoption use. Please contact Berrett-Koehler: Tel: (800) 929-2929; Fax: (802) 864-7626.
Orders by U.S. trade bookstores and wholesalers. Please contact Ingram Publisher Services, Tel: (800) 509-4887; Fax: (800) 838-1149; E-mail: customer.service@ingrampublisherservices.com; or visit www.ingrampublisherservices.com/Ordering for details about electronic ordering.

Berrett-Koehler and the BK logo are registered trademarks of Berrett-Koehler Publishers, Inc.

Printed in the United States of America
Berrett-Koehler books are printed on long-lasting acid-free paper. When it is available, we choose paper that has been manufactured by environmentally responsible processes. These may include using trees grown in sustainable forests, incorporating recycled paper, minimizing chlorine in bleaching, or recycling the energy produced at the paper mill.

Library of Congress Cataloging-in-Publication Data
Mathile, Clayton L.
Run your business, don't let it run you : learning and living
professional management / Clay Mathile.
    pages cm
Includes bibliographical references and index.
ISBN 978-1-60994-895-5 (pbk.)
1. Management. 2. Small business—Management. 3. Organizational change.
4. Strategic planning. 5. Personnel management. I. Title.
HD31.M33737 2013
658--dc23
                                        2013005162

First Edition
19 18 17 16 15 14 13   10 9 8 7 6 5 4 3 2 1

INTERIOR DESIGN: Laura Lind Design   COPY EDITOR: Elissa Rabellino
COVER DESIGN: Richard Adelson   PROOFREADER: Henrietta Bensussen
AUTHOR PHOTO: Pianki Photography   INDEXER: Stimson Indexing
PRODUCTION: Linda Jupiter Productions

This book is dedicated to my heroes—
business owners, whose noble acts of placing
their personal capital at risk and creating jobs
raise the quality of life for all.

Dream no little dreams for they have no magic to move men's souls.

—JOHANN WOLFGANG VON GOETHE

CONTENTS

PREFACE

The greatest myth about running your own business is that you have to do it by yourself. Coupled with the belief that all it takes to succeed is a fierce desire for independence and the willingness to work hard, this myth motivates many of us to roll up our sleeves and do whatever it takes. We focus on the tasks at hand. We're diligent, and we don't give up until the work is done. Sometimes it almost seems easy, taking on its own momentum. From all the effort and dedication, you start seeing results; suddenly you've got the business growing.

Maybe it's grown fast and you're losing confidence that you can keep handling the pace. As it gets harder, you dig in, keep doing the same thing you've always done, muscle your way through. But after a while, that's not enough. You are hitting a wall, or maybe you can see that wall coming. You have an indication or intuition that there's some danger ahead of losing key employees, customers, or vendors, and it feels as if there are other problems on the horizon. You realize that what got you and your business to this level of growth and success won't get you to the next levels. That's disconcerting, to say the least. Something has to shift. You keep thinking that there's got to be a better way.

Your intuition is right. There is a better way, and something does have to shift. It begins with your mind-set—your intentional choice to work *on* your business, not *in* your business. That may be an unfamiliar construct that you can't fathom right now, but it is the key shift. And like turning the right key to open a door, it will help you to forge a new path on which you will set a course for your company and regain the freedom, confidence, and control that you may have felt slip away.

What's Ahead

This book introduces Aileron's Professional Management System for applying and maintaining professional management in your business in a way that works for you. Aileron is a nonprofit organization created to help privately held businesses grow. Professional management is a well-known, established approach of employing proven fundamentals in the running of a business. It is not hiring an outside company to run it. It is learning how to incorporate proven fundamentals—principles and processes—into the everyday workings of your enterprise and applying them to achieve your goals.

Aileron's Professional Management System is based on the principles of professional management as explained by many thought leaders. What distinguishes it is the DOC (Direction, Operation, Control) structure. It simplifies professional management and makes it practical for private businesses. This book is for you, the business owner, unsatisfied with the status quo and eager to better your business, to learn a new way to grow your company. And it is for your team—senior leaders, managers, advisors, and even your family. Our experience is that although you will be the champion of the process, you will want to get the early buy-in of everyone.

Each private business owner has a unique perspective and specific needs. To make it feasible to incorporate professional management, I think each business and each owner needs to start right where you are, identifying a place to apply it in a way that works for you and in a way that solves a problem as soon as possible. There is no one-size-fits-all way to do it. The principles provide a framework, and you adapt that framework as you implement professional management in your business and your life. If you choose to adopt this approach to running your business, I believe that it will be more profitable and successful, and you will have discovered a way to run a sustainable business, just as I did with The Iams Company for many years.

Throughout the book you will meet real business owners, many of them Aileron clients implementing professional management. In our interviews with them, they shared stories of the challenges and fears they faced, as well as the learning, discoveries, and successes they experienced. Their stories won't be exactly like yours, but I think that you will see yourself and your own company's challenges in many of them. They are here because I think it helps to know that you are not alone. There are business owners all around the country who share your heartfelt aspiration for building a successful business that stands for something, and they share your struggles. They understand what you are going through—the real problems you face, your desire to grow your business, the risks you are taking, and the fears you are feeling. They have made the shift, and they are developing vibrant, sustainable businesses through the learning, awareness, capacity-building processes, tools, and support of professional management. Their stories exemplify the ways they have incorporated this system into their companies and the difference it has made in their lives, as well as the lives of their employees, families, and communities. You will meet people like these:

- Tessie and David, whose adoption of professional management has helped them to manage growth, while inspiring innovative controls to ensure high-quality service by employees who love their jobs.

- Christopher, whose company doubled its growth quickly. He was afraid that he could lose it all if he didn't learn how to manage the next wave with timely systems and processes.

- Wes, whose investment in developing his people has resulted in his having the time and the freedom to work on setting the company's future direction and taking family vacations without sacrificing the smooth running of his business.

- Mike and Jeff, who are always balancing freedom and authority with accountability.

- Dan, whose board members helped him learn how to articulate his dream, then strategize a way to achieve it.

- Jim, who worked hard with his executive team to create a strong, authentic culture that drives his business.

- Tony, who incorporated his high-priority value of family into his business culture, which resulted in an invaluable experience for him, for his son, and for his management team.

- Peg and Mark, who needed relief from the 24/7 demands of their business and an exit strategy that would help them meet other goals.

This book is a guide to Aileron's Professional Management System. Part 1, "A Better Way to Run a Business," proposes a solution to the problem of running a business that depends greatly on you in all matters critical to daily operation. It introduces the DOC, its fundamentals, and the shift it requires in your role as leader—stepping back for perspective to look at the bigger picture and to set a long-term direction for the future. Part 2, "Learning Professional Management," goes into more depth on each of the fundamentals, focusing on how you can apply them so that they make sense for you and your employees, and how they can help all of you achieve your short-term and long-term goals. Part 3, "Living Professional Management," is about your intentional interaction with your family about business matters, your awareness of the impact the business has on them, and the importance of a succession plan as part of the legacy and sustainability of your company.

We'll be covering a lot of new ground. As you read what follows, I hope you will experience a shift in your thinking—gaining a new understanding of how critical it is for you to spend the majority of your time working *on* your business instead of *in* it, and beginning to understand the potential impact of professional management. Then I hope you will take a step further and pursue professional management. It all begins with your willingness to shift your focus from the short term to the long term so that you can influence movement in the direction of your vision. I hope that you will begin to feel a sense of what it will be like to be engaged in this process that helps you to get everything going in the same direction. This process isn't easy; in fact, it's hard. You will be challenged to dig deep and to analyze and reflect on a variety of critically important aspects of yourself and your business. But it really works. I believe you will find in this book a sense of something better . . .

a better way to run your business that makes it possible to involve more people and live your values as you achieve new levels of growth, innovation, contribution, profitability, and sustainability.

But my commitment, what drives me to encourage you to pursue professional management, goes deeper. Despite what is happening all around us in the world, I believe in my heart, my gut, and the depths of my soul in the power of small businesses and entrepreneurs as the lifeblood of our communities. To me, nothing is nobler than the business owners' willingness—your willingness—to put your capital at risk to create jobs for others and to invest in the realization of your dreams to grow businesses that stand for something, that will provide a better life for your families, your employees, and your communities. The way I see it, small business is about more than fulfilling the dreams of the owners and their families. You create jobs that give people hope, opportunity, the dignity of work, respect, and valued contribution. Private businesses have the power, one business at a time, to transform the communities in which you do business. You achieve it through personal growth, which fuels organizational growth, which in turn fuels community growth.

NO MORE 16-HOUR DAYS

When Tessie was a young girl, her godfather, a diabetic, underwent a series of amputations. With the help of home health-care professionals, he learned to walk again. Witnessing this process, Tessie was in awe, and it inspired her to want a career in home health care. After working for a home health-care company to gain knowledge and experience, Tessie felt that she understood the inner workings of the business. She was ready to launch her own company.

She got together one evening with her friend David to talk about it. They'd been thinking about this for a long time. That night they sketched out a "business plan" on the back of a napkin and became business partners. Four months later, they were up and running with 20 employees. Tessie said it felt easy in the beginning. "We worked hard contributing everything we had, and the business grew as if by its own momentum. In those years, I don't think we knew enough to understand we were actually running a business. We just went at it knowing we both had enough to contribute. Then it hit us like a ton of bricks."

The turning point for Tessie came with the frightening realization that her business wouldn't continue to grow unless she and David did something differently. What that something was, she had no idea.

> We were successful based on our growth, but we weren't managing it properly. We were not running our business; the business was running us. We needed to change, but we didn't know what needed to be changed or even how to figure out what it was that needed changing. We felt all along that the two of us could make it happen and that we didn't need any help to get through it. But we were feeling exhausted. We were starting to have uncomfortable conversations. We were asking ourselves: "What are we going to do? How are we going to get through the next day and keep up the pace we set for ourselves?" We had just been going on, day after day after day, never taking a look at where we were going. Finally, we hit a wall.

Freedom—Lost and Found

Like many, maybe even most, business owners, Tessie and David were driven to own their business for the freedom it would afford them personally and professionally to be their own boss and to create the kind of quality business they envisioned. Their success in the early stage of building their business didn't prepare them for the struggle to keep up with the pace of growth. Hard work is something you expect, but reaching a point where it feels like you may be jeopardizing what you've built can be scary. Like Tessie and David and many other business owners who have arrived at a similar place 5, 10, or 15 years down the road, perhaps you are thinking, "I don't know how I can keep this up. This is not what I signed up for." Or maybe you can see the potential of that wall coming, and you want to avoid the crash. What gets us to this point?

Driven by a fierce desire for the freedom that owning your own business promises, you jump in, energetically rolling up your sleeves and giving it your all, confident that your knowledge and hard work are all you need. Your dream begins to take shape. Suddenly you have more business than you can handle, along with all the accompanying responsibilities and problems. You are holding on tightly to the belief that you can do everything yourself, not feeling that you can trust anyone else. There's too much at risk. Although it is getting harder and harder, you feel that you have to hold everything together, or it might fall apart.

You fear that if you were to bring someone else in to help you, he wouldn't care as much as you do. Besides, who would that be? How could you find the right person with the right combination of knowledge, experience, and skills, along with genuine caring? He might try to change everything, especially the "secret sauce," the alchemy of ingredients that has made your enterprise unique in your field. You feel alone, stuck, at a loss for how to do things differently. You can't see a way out. You feel trapped. The more you try to manage and control everything and everyone, the worse it gets. Yet it's all you know. You realize that you have to do something differently when something crucial happens, such as one or more of the following events:

- You lose a key employee.

- You lose an important customer.

- Your bank pulls your line of credit or won't approve a loan you need.

- You're having trouble controlling costs.

- You can't hold people accountable.

- You feel the bind you are in; you can't handle the growth you've had, and you need to grow in order to keep going.

- You are tired; you realize that your business isn't good enough to sell, but it isn't bad enough to close.

The freedom you sought by having your own business is fleeting, and your confidence is going with it. Instead, you feel more caged in and stuck in a frustrating cycle. During the day, you are doing your best to keep up with whatever demands arise, while at night you are losing sleep, fearing failure, worried about letting others down, and knowing that all the hard work and determination that got you to this point will not get you out of it. You keep saying to yourself, "There's got to be a better way."

There *is* a better way. I know it will sound ironic to you now, but that tight-fisted control you've been using to run everything, to hold everything together, and to keep it all going one day at a time is limiting your growth potential. It's putting a cap on that potential and locking it down. Although your solo command-and-control style used to work, maybe even was necessary in the beginning, that same tactic won't serve you now that you've grown your business, and certainly not if you want to expand it or sell. You don't have to be the one-man band, doing it all yourself. In fact, if you want to grow, you will need to enlist some other musicians.

When I admitted my own fear, and I realized that I owned the business but didn't know how to run it, my astute wife, Mary, said in her straightforward style, "I guess you'd better learn." I knew she was right. After much reading and research, I discovered *professional management—a way to run a business employing proven fundamentals and disciplines that empower a business to continually reach new levels of growth.* I learned that you don't have to do everything yourself. In fact, if you want your business to grow, you *can't* do everything. You need to include other people—talented, skilled people—and you need to involve everyone: engage them at every level, trust them, and give them responsibility and freedom. *You need to let go instead of holding on so tightly.* This is a big shift—a shift in how you think of your role as the business owner and leader, as well as how you think of the roles of your employees and customers, and of vendors, distributors, and others. More important, it's a shift in how you behave—in what you get up in the morning and do each day.

Professional management helped me to successfully run Iams and to increase sales from $12.5 million to $1 billion over time. And it is helping thousands of others to regain their freedom, confidence, and control, and to run successful businesses. With knowledge collected from some of the nation's foremost business strategists and many owners of privately held businesses who have lived and studied professional management, Aileron has developed a unique system that has been designed to guide and empower private businesses—the owner and the entire organization—to live professional management. We say "live" professional management because it is a values-based system that, once embodied, flows into and benefits your whole life, not just your business.

The system is practical and adaptable, not theoretical. Just the opposite. We want it to make sense to you. And because we want you to be able to apply it right away and be successful, we provide a built-in platform of support. You do the work, but we guide you, help you to find the resources, and hold you accountable. We call it Aileron's Professional Management System, also known as DOC.

We have learned how to distill and teach professional management in digestible pieces. We break it down so that you can learn the fundamentals and implement them in your business. The purpose of the system is to help you get everything going in the same direction and sounding more like a well-orchestrated symphony than a one-man band. This approach helped Tessie and David and thousands of others to discover a better way to run their businesses, and in the following chapters, we hope you will discover it, too.

PART ONE
A BETTER WAY
TO RUN
A BUSINESS

IS YOUR BUSINESS RUNNING YOU?

Wes started his IT business as a way to raise money to go to medical school. He never thought about it as his career or his future until he was in the midst of it. The business took on a life of its own with growth through what he described as "brute force." Wes was energized by every opportunity that came his way. He snapped up every new project despite the pressure that it put on his resources and the toll that all this growth had on everyone. His employees went home drained at the end of each day. Wes knew that he risked losing key people if he kept pushing them, and his family barely had any time with him.

Jim's experience as president and owner of a security services firm had all been growth. He'd never known anything but the upside until October 1, 2008, the first day of his fiscal year, which happened to coincide with the beginning of the Wall Street meltdown and an economic recession. His phone started ringing incessantly, and every caller had the same message: "We need to cut our budget." His company lost 18.5 percent in a matter of months. He had no idea what to do during those market conditions, no experience, no plan, and no one to advise him. He felt powerless and alone. His fears of failure and his isolation mounted daily. Although no one else knew it, he feared that he'd fail to make the payroll. Lying awake most of the night and retreating from his family, he was spending all his time at work worried.

Christopher had doubled his business, bringing it from $10 million to $20 million in a relatively short time. Despite the fact that he was doing well, he feared that he could fail and lose it all. In a way, this fear was a good thing because it was a signal to him to look for help before trying to take the company to the next level. Christopher had grown up in Cameroon, Africa, where, he explained, it was common for the life span of a business to be very short—four or five years—because of a lack of business systems. He was concerned about managing his company's fast growth. Would they be able to make timely changes? Did they have the right people? Did they need training? Was his leadership up to the demands?

Tessie and David, Wes, Jim, and Christopher are like so many business owners who have to experience a big setback to realize that if they want to be sustainable, they can't keep managing their business the same way they have been. Others instinctively know this before they suffer damage. But often, they don't understand why or what has to change.

These business owners aren't alone. Their stories echo those of business owners across the country and around the world. More often than not, business owners find themselves caught in a frustrating cycle of putting all their time, energy, effort, and resources into keeping up with current demands, and this prevents the business from growing to the next level. It's kind of a bait and switch. Much of what you did to build your company to its current level of growth just won't work for you anymore. You've reached a ceiling, or you know that you will if you don't change things before the next wave of growth.

You may already be experiencing some debilitating issues: the loss of a key employee or a vendor, lack of employee engagement, trouble holding employees accountable, or the potential loss of a big customer because of encroaching competition. It is clear that you are not in control, although you work hard to hold on to it. *Despite your firm grip, you are not running your business; the business is running you.* But you don't understand why. You can't step away from the immediacies of the day-to-day demands to get perspective because you don't have time. If you could, you might be able to see that many of the problems you and your employees face are due to a *lack of focus on fundamentals— Direction, Operation, and Control (DOC)*—that can give your business more structure and the opening you need to go to the next level, to be profitable, and to be sustainable.

Setting Direction

When your business isn't achieving what you hoped and expected, do you know why? In many cases, this is because of a lack of clear *direction* for the business. Clarifying direction takes careful thought and communication. Since you are so busy working in the business, doing everything you can to help it to be successful in the short term, you can't carve out any time for the luxury of thinking about and working on a long-term direction for the company. While that would make a big difference, it would take valuable time, and your day is pretty full providing a different kind of direction—micromanagement for employees, customers, vendors, and business partners. You are wearing a lot of hats; there just isn't time to step away to think about the future. With all there is to do, you're feeling lucky to make it through the day without a crisis and relieved that you can keep your head above water.

Setting direction is not only about long-term planning. It's imperative for the short term too. I like to think of direction as a road map for a trip. You need to think *long term* by asking yourself questions such as these:

- Where do I want to go?

- What do I want us (the company) to be when we get there?

But you also need to think about the *short term* and grapple with these questions:

- Who are you (the company)?

- Where are you right now?

- Who do you want your company to be on the journey?

- How do you want to do business while you are on your way?

Setting direction is about being aware of, articulating, and communicating what you do every day, as well as what you want your business to look like in the future. To that end, you need to learn to stretch your thinking by asking these questions:

- How will your business fit into the marketplace?

- How will you provide the needed leadership?

Everyone looks to you, the business owner, to provide clear direction that helps them to know and understand where they are, what they are doing and why, and where all this effort and energy will take them.

You need to communicate all this and create the plans for getting everyone there. In this role of visionary leader, you can involve more people, engage them with purpose, and galvanize them by connecting them to the significance of their contribution in reaching the goal. Without clear direction, you have a group of people with diverse ideas about where to go, what to do, and how to get there. Scattered, maybe even clueless, they have no knowledge or inspiration that helps them to feel motivated by what their work means in the whole scheme of things. They don't know how what they are doing ties into what someone else is doing; they're not aware of what their work will mean to the customer next week or the company in six months or the greater community in six years. Although your employees share space in a building and work for your company, they don't have a real understanding of how everything is connected. Without that sense of purpose and meaningful connection, they can't perform to their fullest potential.

When you feel that you have to do it all yourself and no one else has any idea what needs to be done beyond what's right in front of them, it's hard to work together as a high-functioning team. There is never enough time to do everything that everyone in the business wants to accomplish, and it is hard to identify the highest priorities. Without a long-term direction, employees, vendors, and partners rely completely on you for day-to-day assignments and decisions. They would like to make decisions and take initiative by offering ideas and trying new things, but they don't feel that they can without consulting with you. And so a tightly controlled, frustrating, and self-limiting cycle continues to feed on itself.

It's likely that you don't see or understand how your own behavior, communication or lack of it, and decisions are affecting those around you. At the same time, your employees can't see how their work is contributing to a bigger purpose for the company. They want to know where the business owner wants to take the company so that they can understand how they can make a difference in helping the company to get there.

Having a sense of direction includes understanding how your business fits into the overall marketplace. Failing to understand this makes it nearly impossible to anticipate and respond to changes taking place around you that can influence your business. This can lead to a loss of customers, profits, and competitive advantage, and ultimately to your business being left behind.

Tying In Operations

When you and your business lack direction, the *operation* of the business isn't aligned properly and purposefully to achieve a specific desired result. This causes multiple problems:

■ You assign people certain roles and responsibilities without any parameters for doing so. Often, it is just because they are there or because you think you can count on them, but you don't really know if they have the skills and the capacities to handle whatever comes up.

- As your business has grown, it has been outgrowing the skills and talent of your people, but you don't have time to train them. People may be mismanaged or not managed at all, and you have no way to hold people accountable.

- Employees are not sure how they can contribute and make a difference for the company. They can go only as far as the business owner allows them. If they try to go beyond, they risk getting out of sync with the owner and others. They don't know what they need to do to improve. When they see opportunities for initiative and innovation, they feel handcuffed instead of free to take risks and try something new.

Connecting Controls

In many cases, a desire for greater freedom is a major reason for going into business. Yet in your quest for control, you lose your freedom. In fact, you lose your freedom *and* you lose control. Let's see how this plays out.

To control the results of the business, you think that you have to manage your employees' behavior instead of empowering them to achieve defined results. This mind-set restrains everyone and the business, limiting contribution, innovation, and growth, and making it impossible for you to hold people accountable because there are no stated objectives or standards and no resources provided to achieve them. Everyone's hands are tied.

Sometimes employees can't perform at the level expected simply because they haven't been made aware of the expectations. Employees may need training or resources to develop their potential, to optimize their knowledge and skills, or to learn something new that will advance them and the company. You can find this out only if you measure what is going on in your business—sales, quality of service, customer satisfaction, and anything else that is critical to your company's success in the marketplace.

Controls are a way to measure your progress toward your direction. Establishing controls, or measuring and monitoring results, provides concrete data that you and everyone else can use to understand your current performance and what you need to do to reach your goals. Controls provide clarity. This is not micromanagement of people; it is about measuring and monitoring results. Lack of controls can show up as serious problems:

- Your work culture isn't productive.

- Damaging behaviors, such as apathy, lack of initiative, distrust, disrespect, or negativity appear.

- You have lost touch and are in the dark about what is going on in your own company.

When all three fundamentals—Direction, Operation, and Control—are put into place, all aspects of your business are integrated. You now have a framework in which everything is connected in meaningful ways for *getting everything going in the same direction.* When something shifts in one fundamental, it causes a shift in the others. This inner structure of fundamentals and disciplines is designed to be elastic to allow for growth and change in your business.

Becoming Aware of Your Beliefs and Mind-Set

A lack of direction, operation, and control, with all of its consequences, often leads to a disappointing pattern that might result in burnout for you and your employees, lower client satisfaction, loss of market share, uncertainty on the part of vendors and distributors about your being around for the long haul, lack of backing from your bank, a persistent feeling of being out of control, and a loss of freedom.

The pattern I've drawn is common, and it's usually due to the business owner's own beliefs or mind-set. At Aileron, we see it over and over when people first come to us for help. As you read through the following list of common barrier beliefs, consider whether you are holding any of them. Do any characterize your thinking, and are they part of a vicious cycle frustrating your success?

Common Barrier Beliefs

- You believe that hard work and determination have gotten you this far.

- You believe that if you bring in someone else to help, to take on part of your responsibilities, she will change things and mess up your secret sauce.

- You fear sharing the secrets of your business with anyone else.

- You haven't spent the time to truly understand what you hope to achieve or what you want out of life.

- You are a successor in a multiple-generation family business, and you feel a great obligation to not let the previous generation(s) down.

- ■ You are afraid to ask for help even though you don't know how to break the frustrating cycle you are in.

- ■ You are under the impression that the business is doing well enough until an unforeseen event occurs that throws the business off track.

- ■ The business has grown, but it eventually hits a ceiling, and you don't know where to turn.

The good news is that you can break this cycle. In the next chapter, you will learn more about the fundamentals—Direction, Operation, and Control—and how they can be practically applied to support you and your business. And in the chapters that follow it, we will dive into more detail to help you see how it works.

The fact that you are reading this book means that you can probably identify with many of the problems we have shared. Our hope is that you will soon identify with some of the solutions and find the relief that comes from implementing them in a way that works for you. We hope that you will discover a new way—a better way—to run your business.

CHAPTER 2

SHIFTING TO PROFESSIONAL MANAGEMENT

Professional management—*a way to run a business employing proven fundamentals and disciplines that empower a business to continually reach new levels of growth*, as we have defined it—has been around for a long time. Many books have been written about it by a host of thought leaders who specialize in the subject and express differing viewpoints on its various aspects. Business schools teach it. Management schools do, too. In fact, there is so much information out there that trying to take it in and make sense of it can be overwhelming.

In my early days as sole owner at Iams, as I was seeking the learning I needed to help me, I came across the idea of professional management. I believed it offered a viable solution. I took a course, I worked with consultants, and I applied what I learned. You could say that I became a perennial student of it. Throughout my years in business I've read many books, and I have been most influenced by the theories of Peter Drucker, W. Edwards Deming, Leon Danco, and, more recently, Patrick Lencioni. However, what I learned that has been most valuable has come from putting ideas into practice. Through a great deal of trial and error, I found that some parts of professional management worked better for me and for the Iams organization as we grew. I kept refining and developing our application of professional management as I learned from results and what was happening around me. We crafted a system that worked great for us.

Along the way, I offered my learning to the distributors of the Iams products to help them grow with us. Then, in 1996, I started helping local business owners in our community to implement professional management so that they could reach new levels of growth. Aileron's Professional Management System—DOC—which focuses on privately held businesses, has evolved, and is still evolving, as a result of all this learning and experience and the contributions of many people.

Practical, Not Theoretical

The most important thing I've learned is that you, the business owner of a private business, have unique needs. A theoretical or one-size-fits-all approach won't work. For you to make the shift and then adopt and be successful with a new approach to running your business, that approach needs to be practical, adaptable, and applicable. It needs to work for you, your customers and vendors, your employees, and your family.

You need to be able to put new tools and practices in place in a way that makes sense for you and at a pace that works for you in doable pieces over time. This is how Aileron's system, DOC, has been designed. It is uniquely customized to help each privately held business succeed. There isn't one mold or one path. We break down the concepts and then help you to see how they all connect as a framework and focus on how they are applied. We help everyone involved to make the shift to roles and responsibilities with more impact. This system moves barriers out of the way by helping you to build from wherever you are right now. And the support each step of the way from the facilitators/advisors matches—maybe even exceeds—your own earnest commitment and persistence to do the work. The relentless follow-up and commitment to your success ensure your accountability and progress.

Applying your version of professional management to your business is an incremental process that develops over time. It's a process that is ongoing. You will notice some differences right away, but others will show up after a while. Most people tell us that one of the first differences they notice is that they recover the sense of freedom that they always valued, a feeling of relief and of having more time—time to work on the business and for other things that are important. We think of Aileron's Professional Management System as an integrated, whole approach for running your business and living your life. Because it is an ongoing process with adaptability built in, it has an energy that makes it feel like a living system that frees you to continually learn and grow.

Your professional management system will develop uniquely based on your individual needs and priorities. The fundamentals and disciplines are classic; they stay constant. But every business owner applies and adapts them based on his personal choices. You and your management team will continue to evolve your professional management system over time. You will determine how it is going to show up and shape your business.

Aileron's Professional Management System—DOC—is a living system that is always evolving as we continue to study new business theories and practices and as we work with business owners around the country and discover new practices that work for them. It was developed by business owners who have lived, breathed, and implemented professional management in the real world.

More than 45 years of research and application have proved that business owners who build their businesses with a focus on the fundamentals—Direction, Operation, and Control—are able to successfully take their businesses to the next level. Although each business owner's application is unique to her own business, professional management gives all business owners a common vocabulary and language to use in thinking and talking about it. Having this common language makes a huge difference. It helps you to articulate your own ideas, to communicate and feel understood when talking to others; and having a common language makes it possible to include and involve more people in the process. The language is another tool to foster growth.

Here are an illustration and some definitions for the fundamentals and the disciplines that support them to help you understand Aileron's Professional Management System:

Aileron's Professional Management System

Direction is the ongoing process of establishing and influencing the organization to reach the future desired state or vision you have for it. Direction includes these disciplines:

- *Leadership*, a leader's ongoing process of knowing oneself and developing to become a highly effective leader

- *Strategy*, an organization's ongoing process to prioritize resources aligned to the future desired state that reaches a sustainable competitive advantage

Operation entails aligning the business to achieve the future desired state. Operation includes these disciplines:

■ *Business Structure*, an organization's ongoing method for aligning and allocating the resources and processes needed to achieve the future desired state

■ *People Development*, an organization's ongoing process for growing the individual talent needed for today and the future

Control entails keeping the organization accountable to reach its future desired state. Control includes these disciplines:

■ *Culture*, an organization's ongoing process for fostering the desired environment, behaviors, and organizational beliefs and values

■ *Performance Management*, an organization's ongoing process of monitoring and improving performance

Shifting Your Role and Your Focus

Your new job description, your new role, is to craft the fundamentals (the principles) and disciplines (the processes or methods) for your company. This requires a lot of thought, so thinking and dedicating the time to do so are going to become a big part of your job.

One of the facilitators for Aileron's Course for Presidents invites business owners to imagine this scenario: Someone enters the business owner's office and discovers him staring out the window. "Oh, I'm glad you're not busy," the visitor says. "Right," the owner says, "sorry—I was just thinking."

That conversation not only is ridiculous but also illustrates an important misconception, a necessary shift in mind-set as well as focus. Because you are the owner of the company—the leader—thinking is your job. If you do not take on this work, no one else in your business will. Although it may feel uncomfortable at first and take some adjusting, it will soon feel like the right fit. I've seen how owners who spend time on the fundamentals—Direction, Operation, Control—can learn to think about and live in the future. They can learn how to see around corners and navigate changing markets. By focusing your time on the disciplines—Leadership, Strategy, People Development, Business Structure, Culture, and Performance Management—you can build a successful business.

Your commitment to this role can determine the sustainability of your business. However you describe your role within your company today, you will need to make a conscious effort to change it and to shift some of your current responsibilities to others in your business so that you can create the time to spend on developing these critical areas. Only you can position your company for the future.

Working all the time is an easy trap to fall into. Building a business can be exciting, challenging, consuming . . . even addictive. I confess to falling into that trap. I wasn't able to step back from my crazed way of working until I understood how my role in the business affected everyone else, prevented rather than promoted growth, and had to change. I had to make the shift from being a classic "super-employee" and micromanager to being the leader of a professionally managed business. My focus had to be on building the organization. I had to learn to manage results, not people's activities. Unfortunately, it is easy for business owners to lose focus on their role in the organization and how they need to be spending their time. It's easy to slip back into deeply grooved patterns. The next thing you know, you are doing everyone else's jobs again. You are designing, developing, selling, and delivering your product or service, along with keeping a close eye on the people you hired to do these jobs. You fall into that role of directing and managing behaviors and activities. If this happens, you need to refocus, make that shift and commitment over again, and embed the grooves of a new pattern.

As your employees begin to understand your vision for the business, and as they adjust to this new way of working with you and for you, they will become more confident, innovative, and energetic about how their work can contribute. By getting out of their way and letting them do their jobs, you will be supporting rather than restricting growth. You, your employees, and your business will continually be developing to reach your fullest potential. In addition, you will develop a meaningful legacy expressed by the way you do business that may benefit future generations. It all begins with how you view your role and spend your time.

Shifting How You Spend Your Time

Most entrepreneurs need help making the shift from short-term goals to long-term goals. One business owner, Chris, co-owner of a marketing firm, got the help he needed from an outside board. (We will discuss outside boards in chapter 9.) Like many entrepreneurs, Chris enjoys working in his business. He likes managing projects and getting them done fast, well, and under budget. He gets a kick out of serving customers and loves seeing the swift, measurable payoff. But he also realized that somebody in the business needed to get up out of the trenches and start thinking about the future. He and his partner decided that he would take on the role of chief strategist. This shift was challenging, and it took discipline for him to stop focusing his attention and energy on bringing in and finishing projects and instead to focus on asking whether all the work was getting the company anywhere. Making the shift to working *on* your business instead of *in* the business gives you a way to attain a different perspective, a broader and longer view, and the time for strategic thinking. For some business owners, it is a big relief, a gift, to have the time to do this.

To help Chris stay on track, his board suggested that he log his work time on a spreadsheet for eight weeks, recording hours spent with customers as well as time spent on planning and strategy. Too often, the log showed him slipping back into his old role. It cast his weaknesses into sharp relief, but as uncomfortable as that was, it caused him to grow as a leader. He still gets the urge too often to get his hands into projects, but his new focus on strategy and planning has enabled the business to add new services, form new alliances, and diversify its client portfolio.

Business owners and top managers must let go of the everyday tasks as quickly as possible and focus on their real job, which is to position their enterprise for the future and provide the leadership and vision necessary to get there. This is a full-time job and the real job description of organizational leaders. We see some companies fail because the owners and senior executives cannot make the transition from doer to manager, shifting from being their business's superemployee with a hand in every decision to becoming a leader whose job is to think about the future and where the business should be headed.

How do you make this shift? What does it look like in terms of how you really spend your time and the role you are playing? Usually, it doesn't happen all at once; it's gradual.

Let's say that you are currently making most or all of the decisions in your company. One area that takes a lot of your time and attention is customer issues. You are spending a lot of time, focusing a lot of energy and attention on seeking customers, resolving customer problems and requests, maintaining all your customer relationships. What are some ways that you can change that, shift your role, and still feel confident that your customer issues are all being handled? We'll break it down into three phases. You don't have to do it in three phases; this is just a way to look at how it might be done.

In what we might call *phase one*, you would shift some of your responsibilities to someone else, either someone already in the organization or a new hire. Maybe it's a combination. You would invest time in training and coaching someone else, or maybe more than one person, to take on some customer responsibilities. In *phase two*, you would shift your attention to understanding your customer mix better. You could pay attention to sales data and think about questions like these: Which customers have the best potential for growth? Who pays on time? Which customers are worth spending more time nurturing? What geographic areas have the best potential? Finally, in *phase three*, you would step back and invest your time in thinking about the long-term view: What does my customer mix look like now? What do I want it to look like in the future, five years from now? You could think about how you might manage groups of customers instead of investing time in individual customers. You could set a direction for others in terms of how they might better manage that customer mix.

Let's break down another area that takes up a lot of your time and attention: employee issues. As you transition from being involved in the daily activity of the business to thinking and planning—setting direction—you can play a significant role in establishing an intentional culture in your organization. You can instill meaning, define values, and affect behavior.

In *phase one*, you would take the time to identify and define the values and behaviors that you want to embody and that you want others to see in you. You would communicate those personal values and the values you most wanted to see in your company. You would take time to think about what was most important to you and what you felt was most important in your organization—for example: performance, initiative, fun, speed, respect, teamwork. During *phase two*, you would look for people to hire who held and modeled these values, and you would begin to release people who didn't. Even people who are good at what they do can be what I call "destructive heroes." They create insidious problems that are not healthy for the company's culture. In *phase three*, you would invest in developing other leaders so that they would embody these values and understand them well enough to help infuse them into the organization. They would use these values as parameters for hiring, training, coaching, and developing more leaders in the organization.

The following chart offers another way of looking at the shift.

How You Spend Your Time Now	How You Spend Your Time with Professional Management
Make all the day-to-day decisions	Frame guidelines to empower employees to make more decisions; install systems for delegating responsibilities and accountability
Deal with all clients/customers to resolve problems and maintain relationships	Train a sales manager to develop new business, measure and report on pipeline status; coach others to handle complaints, resolve problems, measure and improve customer satisfaction; analyze your customer mix to determine which ones are most valuable; pay attention to sales data
Deal with all employee issues	Clarify values and develop an intentional culture; hire people who are a good fit; let go of people who are destructive; develop managers and leaders; invest in training programs

If you make the commitment to change your role and shift your focus, you will transition more fully into professional management and its benefits. The shift you make in your focus, away from your current day-to-day responsibilities, will give you greater perspective, and it will shift your company into a sustainable and profitable organization. Your business will begin to see future trends, opportunities, and threats before they are on top of you. You will be able to respond thoughtfully rather than with knee-jerk reactions to changes, and you will be able to avoid surprises and wildfires. This will help your business to become more adaptable and thrive in any market environment. It will become more effective and more profitable. We call this working *on* your business instead of *in* your business.

In the next chapter, we will help you to look more fully at the key points of development for your leadership role.

Reflective Review

Take a little time here and at the end of each chapter to stop and think about the ideas presented and how they apply for you and your business. The reflective review is meant to engage you in the ongoing process of thinking and planning.

- How might thinking about Direction, Operation, and Control help your company?

- How are you spending your time now? Take a few minutes to list what you do in a typical day; or for a broader picture, list what you do in a week.

- What can you see and learn from tracking your daily activity and facing your role as leader? Are you helping your employees to do the jobs you hired them to do? Are you helping to promote growth, or are you unknowingly impeding it?

- What will be the most difficult challenges for you if you shift your role and your focus?

PART TWO
LEARNING PROFESSIONAL MANAGEMENT

CHAPTER 3

HOW YOU LEAD

When Iams opened its first new plant, I took a big step toward letting go by investing in hiring the right manager. I believed we wouldn't be small for long, so with the help of a headhunter, I deliberately hired above our needs. I recruited John, who was managing a plant producing 10 times the volume of our seven-person, one-shift operation.

John was a great hire. He helped us to achieve all of our growth targets and more. But in the process, he had to remind me more than a few times to step back, get out of his way. At one point, he asked, "Clay, when do you plan to let me do the job you hired me to do?" That was a great question, and it jolted me into realizing that I had to break my old habit of forcing my own will and way of doing things on others. I learned that letting John do his job was a way of respecting him. After all, I had hired him for what he could bring to the organization—skills, experience, insight that we didn't have. He was better than I was at some things, and he was overqualified for the present job, but he was equipped to handle the growth that lay ahead. I needed to get out of his way and my own. This was one of many lessons I needed to learn.

Developing Leadership Qualities That Serve Growth

Hiring John gave me the freedom to spend more of my time and effort on planning and developing my leadership capacities. This chapter is about some of the key points for developing your leadership so that you can influence the people involved in your organization and with them take it to higher levels of growth and sustainability. Your process of development as a leader helps you to show up and influence others in ways that help everyone to grow and move forward within a framework that is consistent with who you want to be and what you want your company to be in the world. This is an essential part of setting direction; it's how you keep everything aligned, everyone and everything headed in the same direction. Let's explore some of the leadership qualities that can help you and your business to grow.

Learning and Adapting

Change is hard. It's one thing to say that you want to do things differently, but it's another thing to put new behaviors, policies, and processes into practice. I believe effective leadership depends on a lifelong willingness to learn, grow, and change. I can't think of one quality more important than recognizing that there is always something new to learn that can help you to grow as a person, as a leader, and as a business owner. If you are willing to learn from everything, you'll be more prepared for the evolving capabilities and skills required of you at each new stage of your business's growth. You have to keep learning and growing to keep up.

The best learning often comes from confronting challenges and obstacles, and then asking yourself, "Who has solved this problem before?" You may glean insight from business books or biographies of leaders. Or solutions may emerge in discussions with other business owners, mentors, and advisors. I think that if you make it a priority to seek knowledge, fresh perspectives, and different approaches, you will find that these open up possibilities.

Although many of us are eager to learn about subjects of interest in the world, from birds and orchids to cars, new technology, and presidential history, we often neglect to learn about ourselves. Yet, knowing yourself is the foundation of being a great leader for your company.

Becoming Self-Aware

The biggest obstacle to healthy growth in your business might be a lack of self-awareness—not knowing yourself as well as you think. It's not easy to take a close look at yourself. As a matter of fact, it's hard work. But it's crucial to do the work of answering some tough questions. It is the foundation for everything else. Let's take a little time right now to ignite your thinking.

- What is most important to you?

- What are your values, and how do you want them to show up in the way you work and interact with others?

- How do you want your values to show up in your company?

- What do you believe about yourself and your employees?

- Do your beliefs stand in the way of trusting people to do their jobs?

- Do your beliefs prevent you from reaching for bigger goals?

- Can you identify behaviors that might negatively affect those around you? Can you identify behaviors that positively affect people?

- Are your behaviors holding the business back without your realizing it?

- What are your strengths and weaknesses? Would other people see your strengths and weaknesses the same way?

- What awareness do you have that could translate into a change that might open up the possibility for growth for you and your company?

- Are you willing to change, or do you resist change?

Our experience shows that if you are willing to do the hard work of knowing yourself, digging deep to figure out what is important to you and what you really want, and you are willing to change your patterns, you will be successful as the leader of a professionally managed company.

This means paying attention to how your behavior affects other people and honestly evaluating it. It may mean getting help from coaches, advisors, even therapists if necessary, to see and understand your behavior's impact on others. You will need to regard all feedback from your team and others as constructive—the positive and the negative. This process takes work—practice—every day.

Respecting Others

Learning how to change your behavior can force you to do some of the hardest emotional work of your life. It also will make you a better leader and a better person. One of the toughest changes I made was to stop manipulating people to get what I wanted. With the help of management training, I realized that even though I cared about the people who worked for me, I also tried to mold them to suit my own purposes. I wasn't developing my people; I was manipulating them.

One of my biggest lessons in humility and in respecting others came during a 360-degree evaluation I underwent while in a management training program outside of my company. Before the evaluation, we were divided into groups of five, with four other management peers from other companies, and told to pretend that the CEO of our imaginary company had just been killed in a plane crash. Our job was to pick a new leader from among us.

Determined to be the one chosen, I worked hard to persuade my teammates to select me, and I won the job. Before our second session several months later, we were each evaluated by our peer-group members and also by subordinates at our own real companies. We were also videotaped while working at our own companies. When we returned for the management training follow-up session, we each gave a presentation on what we saw as our own strengths and weaknesses. I tried to make a case that my weakness as a leader was logical thought. It didn't fly.

"Logical thought isn't your weakness at all," said a manager in my group, a savvy grocery-chain executive who had risen through the ranks from the position of checkout clerk. "Your problem is that you use people. You manipulate people to get what you want." She went on to cite an example of how I had told her that she was too valuable in her position as production manager to be promoted. She saw right through that manipulative tactic.

I was stunned, but others quickly agreed, citing other examples. In another jolt, when I reported this to my own management team at Iams, they told me that they agreed with my management training group: I engineered scenarios to get what I wanted.

It was a hard pill to swallow, but after listening to all the feedback, I began to understand the problem. I looked like a good guy on the surface, and while I cared about the people who worked for me, when the pressure was on, I started pulling their strings. I also wasn't getting employees involved enough in our business processes. I was the man behind the curtain directing everyone's actions. My team was standing on the other side, watching and reacting to what I wanted them to see, rather than feeling free and trusted to step up and be proactive participators. My authoritarian behavior threatened to undermine my leadership at a new stage of growth. And it wasn't consistent with who I wanted to be or how I wanted to lead.

Coming to Grips with Your Values and Bringing What Matters to Everything You Do

One of the biggest mistakes that business owners make is failing to figure out what is truly important to them. Knowing what matters most to you helps to give you direction. It helps you to clarify which projects have the highest priority and determine the most valuable way you can spend your time. It is one of the ways that you recover your freedom, feel less overwhelmed, and bring everything into focus. Identifying your values brings your company into alignment with your vision and heartfelt purpose.

Because you are the leader of your company, your values and vision are the foundation for everything that happens in the business. It's important that your vision be clear and that it be grounded in your core values.

I believe that it is in everyone's best interests—business owner, employees, customers, vendors, family, company, and community—to review their values on a regular basis throughout life. At Aileron, we are continually discussing our values and clarifying them. We have eight core values that ground everything we do, all decisions, and our behavior:

- Empowerment
- Living professional management

■ Excellence

■ Development and success of others

■ Collaboration and teamwork

■ The respect of individuals

■ Having a passionate spirit

■ Individuals with virtue

Our values are much more than impressive ideals and words on a piece of paper. We believe that taking the time to reflect on what is most important to us, identifying and defining these values, articulating them, and deciding how we want them to show up is critical to our authenticity . . . walking the talk. We try to embody these values and to live them every day. Aligning our actions with our values is of paramount importance to us. We recognize and celebrate staff when they embody these values, and we hold people accountable when they do not.

Paul Iams, my longtime partner and mentor, embodied integrity. He had a high tolerance for people making mistakes in his company, but he would never accept breaches of integrity. He believed that compromising one's honesty in dealings with customers did irreparable damage. In his words, "It is moral to be honest, but it is also smart to be honest. People remember integrity."

Tony, the owner of an engineering firm, places a high value on his relationship with his family. This is so important to him that he has articulated "family" as one of his organization's values. In his company, people aren't merely encouraged to leave work to attend a school program or to have lunch with a child; they are in trouble if they don't do it.

Scott McClelland, president of a grocery store chain, H-E-B, switched jobs with floor-care employee Donald Lawrence as part of "Leadership Day." He spent the day cleaning floors, wiping down restrooms, and getting to know what it was like to do Lawrence's job. Experiences like this give employees and the owner a broader idea of the entire company's day-to-day operations. It also shows employees that the owner appreciates the contribution of their job and doesn't take them for granted.[1] Respect and appreciation build important relationships with everyone involved in and connected to your enterprise.

Sometimes you have to run your business for a while before you can clarify your values. It was a trip into a convenience store that inspired Norman Mayne, owner of the privately held grocery-store chain Dorothy Lane Markets, to weave respect as a best practice into an overarching mission of highest-quality customer service for his company. It occurred to him that the employee who treated customers poorly was just treating them the way he was treated. So he developed a top-to-bottom value system that guides the company to this day:

- Great service begins with great employees.

- Your employees' first and most effective teacher is you.

- How you hire, train, promote, share information with, and interact with your employees on a day-to-day basis will drive their performance, the quality of your customer service, and ultimately the bottom line.

After Mayne set this in place, his business quickly built a regional reputation for stellar service that was provided by well-trained and well-treated employees whose words and actions reflected the business owner's core values.[2]

Sharing Information and Listening

Aileron's experience with business owners has shown that employees in 95 percent of private enterprises don't know what the owner is thinking. They know the leader wants the business to grow, but she has failed to communicate why and has not articulated the mission and vision in a meaningful way that inspires employees and gives them a powerful feeling of purpose and contribution in their daily work.

Many business owners believe that they're communicating enough, but they're not. Doreen Lorenzo, president of Frog Design, a 600-employee product-design and research firm, says she thought she was being very communicative for some time, so she was surprised when employees asked for more. She began to send out frequent updates, added companywide phone calls, and then started traveling to all the company's offices to hold town hall meetings. She believes that if people are asking for something, a good leader must listen and make adjustments. She even takes time to meet one-on-one with most of her employees because she knows they want to hear the vision straight from her and be reassured that the company has a future. "That's a very human thing," she says.[3]

Failing to share your values and your vision can threaten the survival of your business. Bill Crutchfield, the head of Crutchfield Electronics, founded and grew his company on the principle of listening and responding to customers. He survived in an industry of giants by giving customers user-friendly catalogs and personal service, enabling them to set up and install their new devices themselves. But as the company passed 50 employees, he had difficulty conveying his core values of service and continuous improvement to customer-service reps. These key front-line workers in turn lost their focus and enthusiasm. Growth slowed and sales plunged, pushing the company to the brink of failure.

He sat down and recommitted to paper his core values, which included exceeding customers' expectations and maintaining a passionate commitment to continuous improvement. Then he met with employees, explaining the values and what was behind them. He made it clear that anyone who didn't carry them out would be let go. Not only did the company survive, but its sales grew to $250 million. It scored a string of customer-service awards and thrived debt-free through a deep recession that knocked rival big-box retailer Circuit City out of business.[4]

Walking the Talk

To attract followers, you have to back up your words with actions. It's true that people like to be part of a winning team, but you'll keep your followers even when you make mistakes if you are willing to admit to your mistakes and make them right, and if you're consistent with your message and actions.

I recommend communicating your vision, mission, and values as much as possible, until you get tired of hearing yourself. By that time, the message will be starting to sink in and people will trust that you mean it, especially if they are seeing that you walk the talk, that what you say you believe and think is important is showing up all around them in your company. You can install your vision, mission, values, and beliefs as a living foundation and framework that guides your decisions, actions, and reactions, as well as everyone else's. If you use this foundation and framework consistently and reference it as a basis for your decisions and actions, others will learn to do that, too. If you do not, your employees will not develop the commitment to the foundation and framework, and they will fail to make the connection to it. As you make choices, reference your vision, mission, values, and beliefs; explain how these influenced you. Others will learn to do the same.

Getting Comfortable with Indecision

Wise decision making begins with taking as much time as you can to make the final decision, and it develops through a process of drawing information from a diverse pool of sources, combining judgment with intuition, and tempering optimism by weighing all the evidence. Most of this process, including taking enough time, didn't come naturally to me. Trusting my gut was something I prized. I had to learn to slow down and practice paying more attention to all the evidence available to me. I learned a lot through experience. It might not be intuitive for you either. Perhaps you think debating, researching, and reflecting on decisions is something bureaucrats do. You're uncomfortable with indecision and want to move more quickly, get the tough choices off your plate. But if you can't live with indecision, you are likely to make more mistakes.

The first question you need to ask yourself about any decision is "What evidence do I have to support this?" In the beginning, your go-to response might be "Well, that's my gut feeling." You need to start teaching yourself that a gut feeling isn't good enough. You have to start basing your decisions on evidence, not emotion.

Many business owners equate entrepreneurialism with a speed-and-action, overeager gunslinger mentality. Although some of the qualities associated with this mind-set may have helped you to succeed as the owner of a startup, they are often the same ones that at more advanced stages can cause you to fail. We are much better off tempering our self-confidence and self-reliance with humility and a willingness to listen. Personal drive can blind us to internal problems and market changes.

The best decision makers won't make a decision unless they're sure they understand it. They stop when things seem out of focus. They test opinions against facts. They avoid starting with conclusions. They ask the right questions.

Effective decision makers also weigh opposing viewpoints. Peter Drucker wrote that the best decisions are based "on the clash of conflicting views, the dialogue between different points of view, the choice between different judgments. . . . The right decision demands adequate disagreement."[5] This protects the leader from gambling on a poorly thought-out choice. It also stimulates richer thinking, giving rise to new ideas or fallback plans that come in handy if the original decision goes sour.

Listening to people who disagree with you can be hard when your gut is telling you to act. But it is important to look at problems and solutions through different lenses and entertain conflicting views. By listening to those who won't pander to you, you get a well-rounded picture of all the elements involved in a decision.

Optimism—another common trait among business owners—can be both a blessing and a curse. We think we'll spend less and sell more than we actually do. It would be more prudent to stop before doing a deal and try cutting expected sales volume in half and doubling projected expenditures. It is a good idea to ask, "Would I still do the deal?" If so, it's probably a good idea to go ahead. If not, more scrutiny is required.

Dan, an Aileron client, was excited when an opportunity arose to buy one of the biggest, oldest, best-known competitors in his region—a company three times his company's size. The idea of acquiring a company with that kind of history and name recognition was enticing.

But dissenting views came from his three-member outside board. While the members praised Dan's enthusiasm for trying to tackle such a large undertaking, they cautioned him to slow down. His plan to complete his due-diligence investigation in six months was limiting and too risky. Setting a timeline on such a major decision is seldom a good idea, his board members said. And if a deal is right, it will still be right after taking time for a thorough investigation.

Dan forced himself to slow down and take a deeper look, and it was a good thing he did. He discovered fundamental problems in the business. Moving forward would have been a huge mistake, and this reminded him of an important lesson: just because you can do something doesn't mean you should.

Articulating and Sharing Your Personal Vision

Before you can influence your organization genuinely and meaningfully, you need to clarify your personal vision or dream for everyone to know and understand. One of the first questions I want to ask a business owner is, "Why did you go into business—what are you trying to accomplish?" Then I want to hear the real reason, not just "I thought I could make some money." Every business owner I've ever met has a deeper purpose behind his or her business. Once you articulate it, you can use it as a basis for your company's vision, its reason for being. To me, a vision is a dream with a plan.

Have you ever articulated your dream out loud or written it down? Many people think that their passion or vision is too personal to share. This is another important shift to make in your thinking. Your vision—your dream and personal passion—is far more powerful when you put it in writing, tell people, shout it out to everyone. By sharing it with everyone, you inspire and invite them to become a part of it. Knowing your company's vision can help all your stakeholders connect to their own purpose and to the significant role they play in helping your company to achieve that vision; this can create a powerful synergy.

In a quiet alcove at Aileron called the Dream Room, we keep a leather-bound journal where visitors are free to record their hopes and dreams. What business owners write there has nothing to do with the usual yardsticks of success—big profits, lofty sales gains, or attaining power and position. Instead, they express hope of having an impact on other people in statements such as "to pass on the American Dream to the next generation"; "to be a servant leader and learn to serve others with love"; "to leave the world a little better for my children"; and "to give others the chance to dream."

In the heart of every business owner who wants to be a professional manager there is a desire to build something beyond a large bank account. Most of us want to leave a meaningful, valuable legacy. We want our companies to stand for something. By doing so, we can share that inspiring vision and meaning in our work with our employees, customers, and everyone else connected to us. Long after the money is spent and the business successes are forgotten, we hope that the personal ideals, beliefs, and values we tried to express through our business will be remembered, that they will inspire others and make a difference. Your personal vision can become the lifeblood of the company.

When one business owner started his own software quality-assurance company, he thought of it simply as a way to gain personal freedom and a bigger return on his work. But as the business grew and became successful, he found himself looking for his higher purpose.

He found himself wondering: Why all the hard work? Am I really having an impact? He found his answer by adding up the total salaries he had paid out over the years. The realization that his company had contributed $8 million to the community, providing jobs and prosperity for many families, was a big psychological payoff. He discovered his renewed sense of purpose in the realization of what it meant to be an employer, and this realization became a big motivation for him to continue to improve his management and leadership.

Why not take a little time right now to think about your personal vision. What is it that drives you? What do you hope to achieve? What do you want to build?

Developing Your Leadership as You Grow Your Business

In chapter 2, we looked at some ways in which your role and the roles of your employees shift as you transition into professional management. This is an ongoing process, and it won't look the same for every business owner. I've put together what I call a playbook, an organizational development model that gives you a way of seeing how your role changes as your business grows.

In the startup and early growth phase of your business, Stage I, you can play quarterback, calling and leading execution of all the plays. As the business expands, though, you have to move on and become a player-coach. At Stage II—the "model shop" stage in which the business is making the product well and testing it—you need to take on a coaching role, teaching the game to others but still calling the shots on strategy. Decisions at this stage are made face-to-face, and the climate stays informal. At this point, many business owners still feel compelled to be in control of every decision, and it is still possible at these initial stages to operate that way.

As the business scales up to volume production, however—Stage III—you will need to shift fully into the coaching role, developing other people to play the positions you played before. You need to rely on managers' input for decision making. Technical specialists and more systems, procedures, and budgets are needed.

Organizational Development Model

Stage / Factor	I Proof of Principle Prototype	II Model Shop	III Volume Production	IV Growth/ Decentralization	V Staff Proliferation	VI Strategic Maneuvering	VII Recentralization
Task	Invent and make it	Make it well; test it	Make it and distribute it in volume	Make it profitable		Dominate a niche	
People	Jacks-of-all-trades; risk takers	Jacks and some special risk takers	Technical specialists; non-technical start-up types	Business people	Functional specialist; planners	Planners and strategists	
Reward	Equity; non-bureaucratic climate; make a mark	Non-bureaucratic climate; ground floor advancement	Ground floor advancement; career	Career; salary; bonus (growth)	Career; salary; bonus	Career; salary; bonus (profits)	Career; salary; bonus (asset)
Processes	Informal; face-to-face contact; personal control	Informal; personal contact; meetings	Formal; systems and procedures; budgets; day-to-day operation concerns	Formal control; planning and budget; information systems; control problems	Same as stage IV; more detailed; line/staff problems	Five-year plans; profit center; multi-dimensional plan	Tightening control
Communication/Climate	From leader down/informal	From leader down	From leader down/formal	Internal communication important/difficult	Conservatism slows communication; paralysis possible		Corporate management down
Structure	Informal; little need	Function and hierarchy begin	Functional organization; division of labor centralized	Functional with overlays; division of labor; decentralize	Corporate staff assists leader	Matrix industry/ product profit center; decentralize	Similar to Stage III
Strategy Decisions	Leader	Leader	Leader/ managers input	Made more and more by managers, potential for "loss of control"	Corporate staff assists in decisions	Bottom-up planning	Corporate management
Leader	Quarterback	Player/Coach	Coach	Manager	Manager	Strategist	

Beyond this stage come bigger challenges. In Stages IV, V, and VI, the organization becomes more decentralized, and the business leader-coach must become a manager and eventually a strategist. At this point, many leaders increasingly spend their time developing other people. The staff usually expands to include planners and functional specialists. More formal controls, systems, and plans are needed. Decision making becomes even more decentralized, involving not only other managers but also other members of the organization staff.

Sometimes, no amount of learning is enough to prepare you to lead your business to each new level. In one of the toughest tests of leadership, you may need to admit that you are no longer the best person to run the business. You may prefer to focus on your real passion—research and development or design and production. This choice might be in the best interests of your company, taking it to higher levels of growth. After all, owning a business doesn't automatically mean you need to, or should, run it. That said, if you know what's required and you've examined your own strengths and weaknesses, you'll be in a good position to make the best decision for your company.

Reflective Review

By way of reviewing your personal leadership and your shifting role, let's consider some questions to help you put it all into perspective:

■ Who am I? What do I believe in, and what is important to me?

- What values are showing up in my company? Difficult as it may be, try to be honest about this. What can you do to make sure that what you say is most important to you shows up throughout your company in every interaction?

- Do my employees and customers know what my values are? If I sat down and asked them, would they have different points of view about what is important?

- What are my strengths and weaknesses? How do others see me?

- What impact do my actions have on the organization?

- What are my personal goals?

- What knowledge and skills do I need to learn to accomplish my vision? How will I learn and adapt?

- How do I make decisions? Do I draw information from a diverse pool of resources and give them full consideration? Do I take all the time available to me before making up my mind?

- Is my organization well informed? Am I in touch with my organization?

- What do I need to do to position my company for long-term success?

CHAPTER 4

YOUR DREAM
WITH A PLAN

Strategic planning has gotten a bad rap with some business owners. Perhaps you are among them. You like feeling that you have flexibility, the room to move from one opportunity to another, and you assume that planning places tight constraints on you. You may think that planning strips away your entrepreneurial spirit. There is this misconception that planning means getting your wings clipped, losing freedom, giving up spontaneity and the thrill of the "Aha!" moment. The notion of planning, thinking ahead, and committing smacks of a bureaucracy that you want to avoid, and it seems futile to invest in a weighty plan when the world and the marketplace can change quickly.

In our fast-paced, complex, changing world, it feels as though many things are changing so rapidly, why bother to plan? How can we plan and not feel that our plans are outdated before we put them into action? What good is planning in a global marketplace where things can change in an instant, where instant messaging and instant gratification have become the norm?

Facing a Changing Reality

It is exactly because we live in a fast-paced, complex, changing world with limited resources and innovative technologies that you need to plan for both the short term and the long term. Planning does not place such tight restrictions on you that you no longer have the flexibility to consider opportunities. Another word for planning is *strategy. Strategy gets everyone going in the same direction and keeps everyone moving in that direction, making progress toward your goal.* When an opportunity comes up, you can still put it on the table for consideration. In fact, one of the important strengths of your plan is that you can use it as a framework against which to evaluate the opportunity and make a decision. You might ask yourself the following:

- Does this opportunity fit within our strategy?

- Will it divert resources needed for achieving our goals?

- Does this opportunity challenge any of our strategic assumptions?

Thinking through the answers to these questions along-side your plan will minimize waste of time and resources.

Today, the harsh truth is, if you don't have a plan, you can plan to fail. You need to learn how to see into the future, project, and envision where your company might be in this ever-changing world. But having a plan doesn't mean that it is carved in stone. Plans do shift and change in response to changes in the environment. That is why business leaders need to think of planning or strategizing as something that is ongoing, more of a habit or routine than an activity or a process. Business leaders need to be paying attention, building a deep, broad platform of knowledge, questions, understanding, and discernment. You have to be agile, curious, creative, persevering, and open.

As the world and the marketplaces change, your plans may need to flex and change, too. That's why the best plans derive from a perpetual habit of learning and build-ing your knowledge base. Even if you got your business off the ground without much of a plan, the only way you can turn your dreams for growing your business, making it successful and sustainable, into a reality is by commit-ting yourself to planning as an integral part of your lead-ership and life.

Developing the Habit of Planning

It is critical to your success that strategic planning be-comes a routine part of your life and work. It is through this ongoing process that you determine the direction of your company and its place in the marketplace. *Clarifying, articulating, and communicating your direction to every-one connected to your business is critical to its success and sustainability.*

I am talking about engaging in a thought process that goes much deeper than going through the activities and steps in the typical strategic-planning tool. In the typical strategic-planning session, business owners and facilitators focus on the processes or activities without developing the *habit* of planning and thinking about how certain kinds of information affect dimensions of your business. Although many think of strategic planning as a process, it is really a *disciplined habit of continually thinking, discussing, investigating, communicating, reviewing, and learning.* These are the underlying thought processes that are far more important than what you think of as the traditional process, which is often a project-oriented experience using a tool with steps and activities, separate from and not integrated into a whole approach to affecting growth and sustainability in a more meaningful way.

I have participated in so-called strategic-planning sessions in which the facilitator follows a strict process. The business team members go along with it even though they don't understand the purpose of all the different activities and how the information that comes to the surface will be used. I have walked out at the end of sessions where the team members are frustrated because they don't understand what they have compiled or accomplished. It just isn't meaningful. I think this is a common occurrence and an issue that frustrates many well-intentioned, intelligent business teams.

Often, it happens because the facilitator's focus is on the content—the planning tool and process. He or she isn't focusing an equal amount of time, attention, and preparation on how to make the content meaningful and understandable so that you can absorb it and use it. In some cases, the facilitator wants it to feel complicated and not easily understood so that the business owners and their teams will need them to facilitate. They are invested in your needing them, because that is how they make money. Having a facilitator is a good idea in order to stay on track and to engage in meaningful questions and conversations, but business owners and leadership teams need to understand what they are doing and why throughout the process.

Practical, meaningful application needs to be a thread that is always present. Many tools and exercises are available that can help guide you through strategic thinking and planning. We want to make sure that you understand the application and implications, not just the tools and activities, so that you can determine which will work best for you and your company. A facilitator who does not have anything to personally gain can be invaluable with this. If you can describe what you are trying to accomplish and what you already know and have in place, your facilitator can assist you in determining what tools and exercises will help you to uncover the information you need for a more complete picture. For your growth and the growth of your company, the value is in understanding why this information is meaningful, understanding its implications, and broadening and deepening your knowledge and wisdom.

Planning helps you to define your vision in the context of your reality. This takes practice and tenacity, as well as a willingness to look into the future, to be in unknown territory, and to assess how you want to be part of the future.

Let's look at a couple of questions to see how this works:

■ What are my customers buying from me today?

■ What will these customers want to buy from me in five years?

This is strategic thinking. Somewhere along the line, Jeff Bezos of Amazon.com must have been thinking about these questions and probably many more. Whoever thought at the time, with big-box booksellers expanding, that more books eventually would be purchased online? Whoever dreamed that by 2011, Amazon's customers would purchase more e-books than physical books?[1] In many businesses, leaders have had to ask themselves, "What do my customers want now, and what might they want in the future?" They've had to rethink their business models and imagine new ones. They've had to determine if they wanted to be pioneers— leaders and innovators—or if they preferred to be a part of the market that grows from someone else's innovation.

Steve Jobs and Apple transformed the music industry and the way we listen to music with iTunes, just as it has transformed other industries and parts of our culture with the iPhone, the iPad, and other innovations. We now have an apps industry, which opened up opportunities for new businesses and for expansion in others. Neighborhood grocers offer online shopping and delivery in addition to physical retail stores to better serve their customers. There are multiple ways to rent and view movies. We've come a long way from the local video-rental store, the VHS tape, and the DVD. And some retailers, like Zappos.com and Amazon, offer only the virtual experience—the search, point, and click option. Whoever thought that people would buy shoes without trying them on, without seeing how they felt and looked? Someone had to dream of that. Someone had to envision the possibility, had to want to pioneer and bring the possibility into reality. Others found their place in that market once someone else paved the way. Both approaches require strategic thinking—thoughtful planning.

Because you are the leader of your company, this is your job. It is your responsibility to look into the future and say, "This is where we are going. This is how we are going to get there." Along the way, it is your responsibility to engage others in your organization around your goals and how you will attain them. Strategic planning provides a context for everything you do: developing your knowledge, making decisions, finding focus, refining speed, and using resources effectively. *Strategic planning is the ongoing, underlying, habitual process of thinking, learning, and discerning so that you can continually clarify direction and prioritize resources and strategies to align with your company's future direction.* Staying viable and thriving requires a balance of standing firmly in the current reality while stretching and envisioning your future reality.

Getting Started

Planning is thought-provoking, hard work that takes perspective and time, but it does not need to be complicated. As a matter of fact, I recommend that you start out by keeping it simple. Engage in this new habit by asking some important, basic questions. Get a feel for what it is to be questioning, thinking, and analyzing information, and then thinking some more, becoming accustomed to developing a longer, more expansive perspective. Let's start with a key question:

What is the current reality of your business and your market?

This is a big question. You can break it down into smaller chunks. For example: *What is your internal reality?* Exploring this question invites a realistic review of what your company is. This review evokes more questions:

- What are your strengths and weaknesses as an organization?

- Do you have strong customer loyalty?

- Do you have limited or unlimited capacity when faced with threats or disruptions out of your control? This can be further explored.

  » What are potential opportunities?

  » What do you perceive as threats?

  » Is it possible that perceived threats could be opportunities?

  » What capacity do you have to explore opportunities?

  » What is your capacity to defend threats? What do you need to do?

  » What is your competitive advantage?

  » What is holding your company back?

» Are there strengths that give you a competitive advantage? Would it make sense to continue to invest in and protect that competitive advantage?

» Are there weaknesses that you need to fix? What might be possible if you transformed those into strengths?

Let's stop and think about one of these questions for a few minutes. Can you identify your company's strengths and weaknesses? Write down some notes so that you can really confront them. Do you need help identifying them? If so, engage someone's help. Maybe ask several people's opinions. It is a good idea to get different perspectives, so ask customers, employees, vendors, and your board of advisors, if you have one. Let their input influence your thinking, but you decide based on all the information you gather what you think your strengths and weaknesses are. You can go through the same process with the other questions. You may even think of some questions not listed that would be valuable for you to explore and answer to get a fuller picture of your current reality as a company and your marketplace.

Another part of the equation is your future reality. So, you need to ponder big questions with a longer view:

What is the future reality?

Where do you want to be in that future reality?

These questions invite you to think about your *personal vision* and your *mission*. The first thing I want to know when I work with a business owner is, "Why do you own your business?" I ask, "Beyond making money, why do you work hard? Why do you want to be in business and own this company? What do you hope to achieve?" You may be thinking, "Why does that matter?" It matters big time. It is a big part of articulating your dream.

What Is Your Personal Vision?

Your personal vision is a statement that identifies what you want from your business. Your vision is your dream with a plan. So, clarifying your personal vision, making a statement, helps you to articulate your personal goals, and you can then use these to define and align your business goals.

A personal vision is different from your organization vision. It is really personal. You do not have to share it with anyone, but developing it is extremely helpful in taking the step of articulating your organization's vision. Your personal vision must be clear to you and provide you with a stake that grounds you in making decisions. It can be two or three sentences. The length isn't important as long as it is clear and meaningful to you. Sometimes it takes time to craft, so revisit it often and clarify it until you feel it is solid. Here are some questions you might think about as you work on your personal vision: What do you want to achieve in your life? What are your personal, long-term goals? What meaning would you like your life to have? What contribution would you like to make? Where do you see yourself down the road? What does your vision of the future look and feel like?

When your organizational vision is driven by your personal vision, amazing things can happen. You will be able to maintain a harmony between your personal life and your business, which will lead to more abundant satisfaction. You will be able to monitor your progress toward your personal and business goals, making adjustments as needed. And you will be able to align with what is most important to you, which may simply be creating a better life for you and your family.

What Is Your Vision for Your Company?

Your company vision is a description of what your business will look like in the future, 10 or 15 years down the road. When you write this, use the future tense: "My company will be . . . " Describe it with as much detail and clarity as possible so that it says exactly what you want your company to become. This vision is the ideal state of the business, and it is intended for internal use in your organization. You want every employee to know it and to understand exactly where the business is heading. Note that if your organizational and personal visions are unrelated, you will probably sense that something feels off or out of balance. You might wind up spending too many hours at the office, sacrificing what is truly important to you.

For The Iams Company, the vision was "to be the world leader in dog and cat nutrition." Aileron's vision is "to raise the quality of life in America." One company's vision is "to be recognized by clients, team members, and experts in our industry as the best landscaping company in our market." Another states its vision as, "To be a domestic leader in the residential perimeter security industry." Bill Gates's vision for Microsoft in the first 25 years was "a computer on every desk and in every home."[2] The impact of your vision for all stakeholders can be significant. It is meant to be inspirational.

Scott, a business owner, told us that he thought it would be valuable to see what might happen if the company made an intentional effort to get everyone connected to the company's vision—"Generate perpetual vitality by empower-

ing people and organizations to invest in healthier living."
They often shorten this to "Empowering healthier living."
To do this, they asked everyone to think about what the
vision meant to them, to explain their personal interpreta-
tion. They put up paper on walls in their building, made
marker pens available, and asked everyone to write their
stories of what the vision meant and how they played a part
in it. They left the paper up and the marker pens out for a
long time. It took about two years for everyone to tell their
stories. According to Scott, it was well worth it. They felt
that they already had a pretty good organization, but this
took it to another level. Everyone felt personally more connected to the company's mission and vision; they felt more
committed, and it showed up in results.

What Is Your Mission?

*Your mission is a description of what you do every day.
If you focus on your mission and you do it well, your vision will be the result.* Your mission is a brief statement
that summarizes your organization's reason for existing.
It's typically written in the present tense. It focuses on your
current business and precisely defines what you do. For
example, "We heal people." Or, "To provide sustainable
solutions for energy management in residential and commercial building."

Tessie and David, the owners of a home health-care
company, express their mission in this way: "To inspire
hope and to improve life for those patients entrusted to our
care." Another business owner said that he and his partners defined their mission as, "We help employers take care
of their most important asset—their workforce." Aileron's
mission is "to unleash the potential of private businesses

through professional management." It can take business owners a long time to fine-tune their mission. At Iams, our mission was "to enhance the well-being of dogs and cats by producing world-class, quality foods." It took us a long time to craft that mission. Each year we refined statements, carefully choosing the words we thought were accurate and meaningful. As we crafted our mission statement, we used it to make decisions, important decisions and ones of lesser importance. We only produced foods that "enhanced" a dog's or cat's life. We focused only on dogs and cats and only on high-quality foods. We chose not to expand into related sidelines for pets, like leashes, toys, or bedding.

What Are Your Make-or-Break Priorities?

Setting direction includes getting everyone focused on high priorities. An important question you need to ask in facing your current and future reality is "What priorities do I need to focus on in order to get from here to there?" What are the make-or-break issues that you need to address so that you can attain your vision? You will want to narrow this list down to three or four critical issues, and you will want to make sure that everyone in the organization focuses on them, dedicates resources, and monitors progress. These priorities will guide you in establishing your strategic goals, which we will talk about in chapter 6.

Strategic planning is like a wrestling match that goes on in your head. You aren't wrestling with an opponent; you are struggling with yourself around some key ideas. Now that you have at least started to engage in this process by stimulating your thinking and maybe articulating your thoughts, it is time to bring it all together. There are multiple tools that can help you with this. But basically, you want to look at all your questions and answers and determine what your make-or-break issues are. If you look at your vision, your mission, your current reality, and your future reality, what are the issues that emerge as the ones you must pursue to enable your company to progress toward your vision? It's best not to do this review in a vacuum. Go to some people you respect who can provide different perspectives—valued employees or managers, board members if you have them, and paid advisors. Carefully consider all the information you collect as you come to a final determination.

Reflective Review

You did some thoughtful work while reading this chapter, so give yourself a little time to let it digest now. Go through the following questions, and try to go a step further in your thinking. If you feel ready, write down your responses.

- What keeps you awake at night? What question are you afraid to ask out loud? What are you worried about confronting?

- What information would it be good for you to know in trying to understand clearly who your company is and how it is perceived in the marketplace?

- What is your personal vision?

- What is your mission for your company?

- What is possible for your company in the future if you are achieving outstanding results in your market? Think of this as your future vision.

CHAPTER 5

GROW YOUR PEOPLE, GROW YOUR BUSINESS

eople are your most valuable asset, so it makes sense that one of your most important roles is to develop them, each and every person individually, as part of teams and as an essential part of the organization. Investing in your employees by expanding their responsibilities, giving them opportunities for new learning, encouraging them to set goals and have development plans, providing coaching and feedback, and holding them accountable will build trust, commitment, and passion toward your mission and vision. *A committed, passionate workforce will deliver your long-term business goals and move you closer to realizing your vision.*

This chapter explores ways in which you can tap into your employees' talents and unleash their potential in ways that can mutually benefit the employees and your business today and in the future. People development is essential for operationalizing your strategy.

Growing Talent

The commitment to developing people needs to be a high priority. It is so significant that it needs to be a central focus, with a goal of building the best workforce in the industry. This is a collaborative process that fosters an intersection of the needs and desires of individuals with the current and future needs of the company as it grows. In fact, the more intertwined this process is, the more likely you are to be successful at building a truly sustainable enterprise, because it is through this process that individuals see and feel the connection of their own passionate purpose and valuable contribution with the mission and vision of the company.

Collaborating on Goals and Plans

The process for growing your individual talent begins when you or your managers engage in discussion with direct reports to understand each employee's personal and professional goals and how these goals align with the current and future needs of the business. Working with managers to establish development goals and plans, the employee takes ownership of his or her personal development. The managers coach, provide feedback, and provide opportunities for learning experiences and new challenges that offer growth.

Managers can learn a lot by talking with employees about what interests them. Then, as business goals are defined and roles and responsibilities are clarified, it is up to managers to ensure that individuals have the opportunities to develop their knowledge and skills in areas that interest them. This is part of their partnership or collaboration. It is of mutual value to the individual and the company because people who are doing what they enjoy and what is exciting to them are more productive.

A few years ago, a company decided that it needed to solidify its brand. They didn't have anyone on staff who had expertise in branding, but they did have an employee who had expressed an interest in learning and developing in this area. Instead of hiring a new employee, they identified potential training opportunities for the enthusiastic employee to pursue. Then they hired a consultant to work with her on the rebranding project. The employee took the development opportunity seriously and learned a great deal in a short time. The rebranding efforts were successful, and now the company has an individual on staff who has this knowledge. The employee feels an even stronger dedication to the organization because she appreciates the development opportunities that she was given. As your operational plans unfold, look for those prime opportunities for your people to develop in new areas that align with their interests and the organization's needs.

Involving employees in discussions of company goals and plans enhances their feelings of being valued. If you are listening and considering what your employees have to say, especially because you genuinely value their experience and insight, they will feel highly valued and take very seriously your respect and trust—and, more important, the significance of their responsibility and contribution. This gives the employees another reason to feel that they have a real stake in making contributions toward the goals and vision of the organization.

Investing in Training and Development

We consider it a best practice to invest heavily in meaningful training and development. Not merely events that are a break from the work routine (although celebrations can be good for morale and need no other purpose), but real learning experiences that engage people, help them to develop knowledge and skills, stretch them and catalyze their freedom to innovate, enable them to assume more responsibility, and take them to increased levels of contribution. People want to develop their knowledge, skills, and value. They become energized by the growth, and they want to contribute in meaningful ways. Helping people to grow, achieve their personal goals, and be their best is a way of caring about them—respecting them—that they will highly appreciate. Feeling appreciated will in turn galvanize them to work hard and want to add real value to your business.

Developing Managers

Create a system for individuals to become successful managers. As your organization grows and you need to install a new level of management, these skills need to be developed. This isn't always easy. Typically, what got people promoted to supervise or manage is their mastery of technical skills, not typically their management skills. These need to be learned and developed, usually through training, mentorship, and coaching, because working through others can be unnatural and challenging. However, it is essential for a growing organization, and once you've gotten the hang of it, it can be very rewarding. Help your people to become effective managers. Invest in their learning and success. Help them to see that they are contributing more by developing others through these new management skills.

Developing people, individual contributors and people who want to be managers, is the single most important benefit to employees, next to getting fair financial compensation. When your people know there is a path for them to add to their knowledge, skills, and expertise, a path that provides ways for them to expand their role and responsibilities and take on new challenges, they will strive and thrive, and so will your company. As your company grows, you will want to add a process for management succession, so that people who want to move in this arena by taking greater responsibility can do so and are aware of how to make that happen.

Delegating Responsibilities and Developing Leadership at All Levels

Delegating is often a big stretch for all of us. But it is a lot easier to let go and give others responsibilities when you provide the boundaries for authority and decision making, or "the area of freedom." We sometimes refer to this as the "sandbox."

Imagine a square structure framed by each of these four areas:

Side one—Values that are core to your culture

Side two—Policies and procedures for your company

Sandbox—Area Freedom

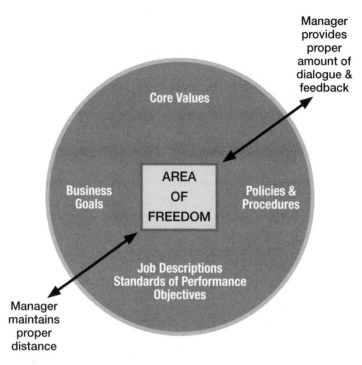

Side three—Job descriptions and standards of performance objectives that describe what the work is and what must be accomplished

Side four—Business goals

Defining these boundaries makes it clear to employees where they can operate with a degree of freedom. To respect this freedom, you and other leaders and managers need to maintain a respectful distance along with appropriate dialogue and feedback. You will want to encourage people to push out the boundaries. This process challenges employees to ask for more authority and to promote continued growth.

Here's an example of how the *sandbox*, or *area of freedom*, can be practically applied. A sales manager for a technology firm described the boundaries of his sandbox as follows:

Values (side one)—Excellence, individuals with virtue, teamwork and collaboration.

Policies and procedures (side two)—All quotes are developed and agreed upon by sales manager and project team before being presented to client.

Job description and standards (side three)—He is responsible for relationships with all new customers. He

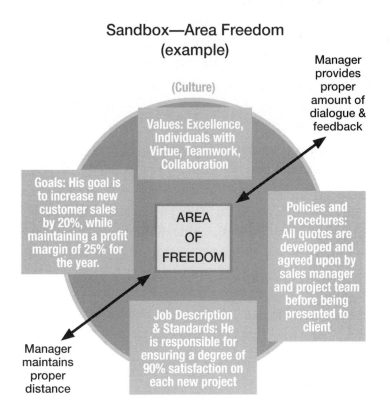

Sandbox—Area Freedom (example)

is responsible for ensuring a degree of 90 percent customer satisfaction on each new project.

Goals (side four)—His goal is to increase new-customer sales by 20 percent while maintaining a profit margin of 25 percent for the year.

Having these parameters of authority makes it easier for this sales manager to make decisions and handle customer requests. Here's an example of how they can give him freedom and guidelines in making real-life decisions in a difficult situation with a new customer. The clients ask the sales manager for a quote on integrating two technologies. His team has extensive knowledge and experience with both technologies and wants to offer a different solution to the clients because they already know that these technologies do not work well together. This is a big project, and it would help the sales manager to hit his goals. The clients aren't open to listening to an alternative solution. They keep pushing the sales manager for a quote on integrating the two technologies, which he knows will only mean problems for them. He could give them a quote, and his company could do the work, but it doesn't feel right. The sales manager knows that the clients will not be happy with the final solution, and although he would meet his goals, the longer-term cost to the company would be too high. The sales manager knows that each project reflects the company's values, and he is responsible for reflecting the value of excellence. He knows that the project requirements as designed by the clients will not result in a successful solution. Therefore, the sales manager chooses to communicate honestly with the clients to explain the reasons why his firm has decided not to offer a quote on the project.

The clients were frustrated and disappointed at first. But eventually, they understood the problematic nature of the technology issues that the sales manager was describing, and they asked the sales manager to propose another solution.

Without the sandbox, the sales manager could have proposed a quote for the job, the firm could have done the work and charged the clients, and the clients would have gotten what they requested, but they also would have been dissatisfied. They likely would have expressed their dissatisfaction to others and complained of the poor-quality work by the firm, which would have damaged the firm's reputation. The sales manager would have met his goals for the year and probably received compensation for doing so. However, this would have happened at great cost; it would have been a shortsighted decision.

Pushing Down and Spreading Out Decision Making

The people on the front lines, like the sales manager you just met, other managers, and individual contributors, are the ones closest to what is going on every day. They need to have the freedom and accountability to make good decisions. They are in a position to notice things, even small things, that can make big differences. Too often, good ideas from the front lines are suppressed or wasted because people don't feel empowered to voice them, bring them to anyone's attention, or take initiative to develop them.

When I worked as a purchasing manager at a big packaged-food company, a veteran maintenance supervisor named Ernie had figured out a way to save a lot of money. He quietly began substituting nylon rollers for steel rollers on the track that moved products along the production line. He was working under the radar, because this improvement required him to break both government rules and internal company regulations requiring stainless steel rollers. But the nylon rollers lasted ten times longer and reduced wear on supporting parts.

Ernie's quiet little innovation was saving the company $60,000 per machine per year, but he was afraid to ask for management approval because his idea broke the rules. I was a purchasing manager at the time and helped him by persuading a government inspector to OK the change and by reporting the savings to management. Executives at the company picked up on the idea and other plants adopted it. The company saved $1 million a year thanks to Ernie, a guy who knew the production equipment better than anybody else but had no voice in the company.

The front lines are where good ideas need to flourish and decisions need to be made. *Smart business owners train and empower everyone to make decisions that serve the company's strategy by providing some guidelines and frameworks, like the "sandbox," to encourage innovation and leadership at all levels.* People need to feel that they have the freedom and authority to speak up, to solve problems and pursue ideas. People need to have a clear sense that ideas are welcome and there is a pathway for moving them through the organization so that they can be recognized, implemented, and optimized. This needs to be encouraged and rewarded at all levels and in every nook and cranny of the company. *Leadership can come from anyone anywhere in the company* because of their expertise in their area, their awareness, and their initiative, and because they know that they have the freedom and authority to pursue a good idea. There is a difference between management or positional authority and pure leadership. The wisdom of the decision has nothing to do with the power of the position.

The implications of spreading freedom and accountability through the organization are transformative. Wes, owner of an IT firm, took a long-needed two-week vacation with his family. When he returned to work, he went to his desk to handle everything that required his attention. He expected to find a stack that would take days to dig through. Instead, he was finished in a day and a half. Then he realized that he didn't have anything to do. His desk was clean. For a few minutes, he felt a sense of sheer terror. Before implementing professional management, that kind of lapse in activity for him would have meant his business was in crisis. If he didn't have anything to do, that meant his company didn't have anything to do. This time around, he realized, it was a signal that everything was going exactly as designed. His managers and other employees were well prepared to assume more responsibility and make decisions. His desk was clean because his employees were doing what they were supposed to do.

Learning to Hold People Accountable

A common complaint from business owners is that their employees are not accountable for their work. Or they believe that their employees don't work hard enough, put out enough effort to help the business to be successful. But when we ask business owners, "How much more is enough? What exactly do you want from them?" they can't answer those questions clearly. Instead of negotiating goals and clarifying expectations, many business owners tend to assume that their employees already know what is expected of them. This is a big mistake, an incorrect assumption, and it creates a gap or, even worse, a misunderstanding in your relationship with your employees. Most important, it doesn't serve you, your business, or your employees.

To bring out in your employees the desire to work hard and help the company to succeed, you need to talk with them. Discuss your expectations and listen to theirs. Try to bring both into alignment so that everyone feels there is a mutual understanding and a satisfactory relationship. I've found that most employees want to contribute and to be successful; they just need direction and clear communication on what is expected. Many genuinely want to exceed expectations, but they can do so only if they know what those expectations are, if they are defined and agreed upon. I know it's a cliché, but we're not mind readers, and neither are they. We need to say what we want and expect in order to give people the opening to be all that we hope for, and maybe even more. (We will discuss accountability further in chapter 8.)

Receiving Feedback as a Gift and Offering It with Respect

A long time ago, a mentor of mine told me that he had a gift for me, and he asked me if I wanted it. Somewhat confused, I said, "Sure." He went on to explain that this gift was feedback on my behavior. "It might not feel like a gift right now, but if you choose to accept it, someday you may understand why I am calling it a gift."

I did choose to accept my mentor's feedback, and I did understand its long-term value to me as a person and as a business leader. I also learned to view the giving and receiving of feedback in a completely new way. Only people who really care about you and your development are willing to give you the gift of honest insight on how you come across and interact with others, and we all need someone with the courage, perspective, and good sense to do that in a way we can accept. I have learned to welcome feedback as a gift, to appreciate it, to say thank you and give it proper consideration. This took a bit of adjusting for me. I had to move my ego out of the way to view this as an opportunity for learning, to see it as the gift it really is. It's always been valuable for me, and I would like to pass this perspective on to you.

You will gain a lot by being open to and appreciative of hearing honest feedback. Your reaction, or what I've learned to think of as a more thoughtful response, at these moments will affect the quality of the feedback you receive from others, as well as their willingness to approach you again.

There is an art not only to receiving feedback but also to giving it. My mentor approached me in a way that made me feel safe and open to it. Of course, I also trusted this person. I've learned that an important part of the giving is being respectful and honest in the process. You want to communicate to the receiver that you care, that you want to help that person to become a better version of herself or himself. If you have insight that you believe will be helpful and you don't offer it, ask yourself why. Are you afraid to have what might be an uncomfortable conversation? Are you not willing to put out the energy and effort? Do you need to learn how to have this kind of conversation? Perhaps you need training and practice; many people do. If so, seek it out and learn this valuable skill. Whatever the reason, if you are avoiding giving honest, valuable insight, you will want to overcome whatever is holding you back. You will be a better leader when you can offer meaningful feedback.

Building a Strong Leadership Team

By now, I think you understand that the growth and sustainability of your business depend on the development of everyone in the organization. An important phase of growth for you as a leader of a growing, professionally managed organization is to include more people in leadership—to develop the next layer, a strong, cohesive leadership team that you can rely on to help you take your company to the next levels of growth. This can be a huge challenge, but it is well worth the energy and effort. The individuals on your senior management team may not have the experience of working together and feeling that their first loyalty is to the team. It is likely that they are accustomed to working with a silo mentality. Their loyalty has been to their department and their departmental teams. It's a big shift for them to develop trust and loyalty to this new team.

That can come only from your leadership, getting them to work together, to learn that they can count on each other, to have the experience and the feeling that they are solving problems together and that they are part of the same team. This takes time. The organization must have trust in the entire leadership team and see it as a cohesive unit. All the employees must trust that expectations between departments and throughout the organization are consistent and aligned with values.

When you have a solid team, you can let go of day-to-day operations with more confidence. You can shift more into the long-term planning that is necessary for your company's future growth. This is good for everyone. Your team will want to support you in your role by doing their jobs to the nth degree, because they understand that it serves everyone within and connected to the company for the company to grow and be successful. Your leadership team will rally around you and your goals. They will take on these goals as their own and communicate them to the rest of the company, who will carry them to your suppliers, distributors, customers, and the greater community. Your leadership team can help everyone connect to the values and the culture, the mission and the vision—the role each person plays in contributing toward the growth and success. A great leadership team can help you to drive support at all levels of your company by making sure that everyone is engaged and accountable.

How do you build a leadership team? This begins with looking for and assessing talent, seeing people as leaders, and discerning what they need for growing into the role. You might find some people right under your nose, and you may need to reach further to bring in the talent you require. You will want to surround yourself with people who have varied assets. I believe it's important to seek people who have knowledge, skills, talent, and experience beyond your own, as well as people who complement what you bring to the table. As you build your team, look for people who can be team players, who are respectful and trustworthy, but also who are unafraid to question decisions, challenge ideas and solutions, bring forward diverse approaches and perspectives, and encourage taking some risks, experimenting, and trying new things. You want your leadership team to be made up of people who listen well, believe in the value of continual learning, want to keep developing, and will help others to do so. You also want your leadership team to be committed to helping everyone succeed—to working together collaboratively in support of common goals and the greater purpose.

Reflective Review

- Do people understand they are expected to stretch, to learn and to grow continuously?

- Do you, your leaders, and your managers know the personal and professional goals of your direct reports? Are your employees involved in a collaborative plan that aligns their development goals with current and future company needs?

- Do your employees feel ownership in current and future plans? Would your employees say they are empowered to achieve the desired results?

- Are those closest to the work involved in defining the systems and the processes? Are they responsible for the outcome? Do they have the authority to make decisions?

- Do employees know and understand their boundaries for authority and decisions?

- Do your employees receive regular open, honest, and transparent feedback?

- What do you know about your employees? Do you know what interests they have outside of work that could be leveraged to achieve company goals?

- Do you know the individual and collective strengths of your direct reports? Do you leverage the individual and collective strengths of your employees?

- What drives or motivates your employees? What detracts from your employees' motivation?

- Are your employees connected to the company's vision and mission? Can they articulate it, and do they feel connected to it? Are your employees committed to a common goal and to achieving results?

CHAPTER 6

ALIGNING YOUR BUSINESS WITH YOUR VISION

Having a strategy with goals and priorities with which to set direction is only part of the equation for professionally managing your business. That's why the O (Operation) in DOC includes Business Structure. The heart and guts of your business is the structure you create that helps people bring your vision to life. Having an intentional business structure is *organizing your business in a way that helps everyone to be successful.*

So, what is business structure? How does it help you and others in practical, meaningful ways? I think of it as the who, what, when, where, why, and how of business. It brings together your vision and mission with the people and the work. It operationalizes your goals. An effective structure reflects how decisions are made, how work gets done, how roles and relationships are defined, and where boundaries lie among departments and people. The goal of a good organizational structure is to provide a framework for putting your business's strategy into action.

In this chapter, we will discuss structure in these forms: business model, operational planning, organizing people and work into areas of responsibility, and performance standards. We believe that intentionally developing these structures or processes is practical and meaningful in achieving growth and sustainability, and it plays a huge role in making sure that you are running your business instead of feeling like your business is running you.

Setting Up Structure to Align with Strategy

Jay was a great salesman, a top achiever, highly motivated and hardworking. He liked nothing better than selling his products, and he was loyal to the company. He had started working for a wholesale wine-distributing company right out of college, and he hoped to move up through the management ranks, but he had one big problem. He didn't like navigating systems and processes, the paperwork and reports that went along with the responsibilities. He just liked to sell and motivate others to sell. He considered policies,

standards, and reviews cumbersome, meaningless, bureaucratic red tape.

When he left the company to start his own business
with Larry and Tim, two friends he'd met early in his career, who worked in finance and marketing, he vowed that
he wouldn't have anything to do with all that bureaucratic
stuff, but Larry and Tim pushed back. They insisted that
it would be a big mistake and that it would place the company at high risk. It took some convincing, but Larry and
Tim, who were more experienced, made the case for putting some structure in place from the beginning by promising Jay that it didn't take any of the freedom out of owning
his own business—as a matter of fact, it helped to secure
that freedom—and it made everyone's jobs clearer and
more meaningful by connecting them to short-term and
long-term goals.

Like Jay, many business owners think of structure negatively, as something that is "too corporate." But putting in
frameworks empowers people and organizations to thrive.
We aren't talking about a bunch of rules and regulations or
charts for the sake of theoretical exercise. *Structure is looking
at how you have organized your business so that it will produce the results you want.* Ask yourself: Do you have a compensation structure that rewards the behaviors you want? Do
you have a business model that meets the business's strategic
needs for the future and the customers' desires? Do you have
an organizational design to best serve the goals?

Your organization will develop a structure whether you
manage it or not, and when structure is left to grow on its
own, the results can be dysfunctional. A common scenario
is that companies develop a centralized control structure

that works less and less well as the business grows. This setup is dysfunctional because nobody ever gets together to set objectives or compare data, and the business owner is the only person who knows all that's going on. This structure fosters distrust and silos. The business owner can't see the bigger picture because he is consumed with one-on-one communications with many people.

I can't make the case strongly enough for intentionally developing and managing your company's structure so that it aligns with your strategy. Meaningful structure creates focus and keeps everyone on track, preventing you from wasting resources on non-priority issues or high-risk projects. It is this combination of strategy and business structure that optimizes your vision.

Mike and Jeff, co-owners of a manufacturing company that has been thriving for over 120 years, say that you don't survive that long without structure and controls. (Controls are part of operationalizing your structure, and we will discuss this in chapter 7.) They are proud that when the recession hit in 2008, they didn't have to lay off a single person. They credit multiple structures they had in place, including budgets and financial review processes in which they are always keeping an eye on cash flow, forecasting it, and maintaining a conservative cushion. At the same time, they are making investments and taking risks, some greater than others, but they are always calculating these investments and risks for high probability of success. They have structures in place for holding people accountable, monitoring high-risk projects carefully, and pulling the plug early when that's the right call. They talk over and over again about continually trying to balance freedom and authority and risk management with accountability processes. The only way you can do that is if you have structure in place to define, guide, and set limits.

Another important reason for framing up structure is the value it brings to your organization. One business owner turned to professional management for help after unsuccessfully trying to sell his business. His accountant and attorney recommended that he build structure into his business to increase its value. The only value that potential buyers could see in his business was him. The business was dependent on his being there, making all decisions and running the day-to-day operation.

When an organization is set up effectively with structure, it should be able to continue to run regardless of the owner's presence. You should be able to take extended periods of time off without worry. People should be able to see you as replaceable, and if you want to sell it, potential buyers should be able to see that the company is not dependent on you. Having an effective structure makes it much easier for someone else to envision coming in and taking over. An accountant, a lawyer, and anyone who might want to buy your business will be able to see easily the value of your company because of your strong business structure.

What Is Structure?

Structure is everything you do (or choose not to do) to connect people to your goals. This includes the following: establishing operational goals, setting up policies and procedures, defining projects and services, creating a budget and processes for allocating resources, compensation and bonuses, revenue streams, the way your organization functions in terms of authority and connection, the way you organize your people into jobs and areas of responsibility or departments, having a business model, and more. Working collaboratively and effectively, your people have a good idea of what it takes to meet or maybe even exceed goals. To quote one business owner, "Structure is the basis for satisfaction by all stakeholders—owners, customers, and employees. Employees feel empowered and successful as the company thrives."

Structural components take time to think through and develop, but once in place, they provide invaluable guidance for more freedom, authority, and accountability. For example, many, maybe even most, businesses start out without drawing up a business model, an important structural foundation that defines your business and its value. Although businesses can operate and grow without a business model, they can do so only to a certain point. Usually it is because of the lack of a carefully crafted business model that they hit a ceiling.

If counterproductive structural elements exist in a company, these do need to be acknowledged, reviewed, and revised because the purpose of structure is to facilitate the work and progress toward goals and growth, not to thwart it. *The rubber meets the road when you involve the organization by aligning the structure of the business to reach the desired outcomes. Your structure helps make sense of how everything is connected.*

Developing a Business Model

A business model is a powerful tool for defining your business and how your business works to create value. It is a document you create that succinctly defines foundational business components. It can take a period of time, as long as a year or more, to think through these definitions and clarify them. You might want to work on this with an advisor to help you develop your thought process. Once you have crafted your model, you will want to keep reviewing and refining it. You will also want to share it with your team and maybe others. Everyone involved in decisions that have to do with how the business operates and how it creates value can use it as a basis for decisions.

Presented here are the components of a business model with brief definitions. These are based on a well-known, free tool called Business Model Canvas.[1] It is a good idea to begin thinking about these components and definitions, and when you are ready to develop your model, you will have a head start. It is so crucial to growth that you will want to make sure that you give it careful consideration.

Components of a Business Model

Key Partners—In this frame of your model, you name people or groups that you view as partners in your organization. You define the relationships between your company and people outside the company by defining the level of information to be shared, the level of trust that can be assumed, and the nature and purpose of those relationships.

Processes Critical to the Organization—It is important to name and define the top five to seven critical processes that help your organization to understand its boundaries and expectations. If you name strategic planning as a critical process, that communicates to the whole organization your commitment and expectation that everyone will understand that process, as well as their role in the process, so that they can do their best to follow and continuously improve it. Other critical process areas are communications, product development, project management, hiring and onboarding, continuous improvement, employee development, and management succession. Defining the critical processes for your organization brings them into focus for your organization and identifies them as priorities that everyone needs to consistently commit themselves to using and mastering.

Pricing Model and Cost Structure—Definition of your pricing and costs provides important guidelines for the organization. It helps people to make decisions on how to price products and services and how to manage various expenses. It protects your market position. It helps your team to make decisions on quotes to customers and guides their communication with clients regarding your price and the value.

Value Proposition—This is sometimes the most difficult for businesses to define. Think of it as the way in which you create value in the marketplace. It is best expressed by answering the following questions: What is it that really makes you distinct and valuable to your customers or clients? Why does it distinguish you? Why is it valuable? How do you maintain it?

Revenue Streams—Defining your revenue streams helps your organization to understand where they need to go to generate revenue. It provides focus and clarity and minimizes wasted resources.

Key Channels—In this part of the model, you define channels or areas where you find new clients. If you own a dry-cleaning business and your target market is business professionals, you might market to professional trade associations. Clarifying key channels helps you determine which ones to pursue within your target market and how your organization will pursue them. This provides direction to your team, as well as alignment and consistency in your efforts to build your client base.

Customer Relationships—This is your clarification of how you work with clients. You can clarify these relationships by answering the following questions: What do you do? What level of service do you commit to for your customers? Who are your customers? What can they expect from you?

When businesses put off consciously creating a business model, there can be drawbacks in addition to limiting growth. Over time, a business might find that it has been using several models, never really committing to one. This can happen because the company is being opportunistic, pursuing many different avenues, which can make things unnecessarily complicated and dysfunctional. Your business model is meant to make things clearer. When you and your organization know and understand the components of your model, you will be able to see if it will produce the results you have defined in your strategy.

Operationalizing Your Strategic Plan

It's one thing to have a great vision and a plan with strategic goals; it's another thing to make them real and operational. The structure of your business can encourage or prevent the flow of information. Regardless of how good your business strategy is, an ineffective business structure can keep you from executing it. An effective structure is balanced. It promotes communication, eliminates barriers between teams, and clarifies individual roles and responsibilities.

The only way for you and everyone else in your business to be accountable and be part of the effort to make progress toward your goals is for you to set up a control process. This is the structure or process in which you establish various levels of goals throughout the organization, making sure that everyone is part of the process, measuring and monitoring the most relevant information required to review progress toward those goals.

This is operationalizing your strategic plan. The process has two components: *operational planning*, which is setting goals, and *performance standards*, which is the process of setting up standards for success in each area of responsibility. The process includes reevaluating goals, making adjustments as needed, and engaging everyone in realistic conversations, feedback, and new ideas while working to meet and possibly exceed expectations. Setting goals and establishing performance standards is the way you connect daily work to your short-term goals and your future vision.

The business owner must integrate the strategic plan into operations. This takes time and needs to be a high priority. The owner of a technology business says that developing a strategic plan has been a straightforward process, helping him to define his market for the first time and assess where the company is, where he and his team want it to be, and how they can get it there. But execution has been tough. Motivating his people to align operations, controls, and employee pay and incentives with the strategic plan has been a major challenge. Some employees haven't been able to handle the changes and have been let go. The business owner has been setting milestones of one to three months, but he's falling short in following up with individual team members, evaluating their progress, and defining next steps. Nevertheless, he feels that he's starting to work *on* his business, rather than *in* it, and results are closer to plan with each passing year.

Operational Planning

Operational planning starts with your long-term strategic goals. Once you have established these, you want to make sure that they become woven into the daily work of every person, team, group, and department in the company. This cascading of goals through the organization is the first step in establishing priorities. It breaks the big goals down so that every manager, department, group, team, and individual contributor takes on a piece of that goal in connection with her contribution. Here's a more step-by-step view:

> *Phase* 1—Identify your organization's operational goals. These are goals that can be measured monthly, so if you are meeting them monthly, you know that you will meet your strategic goals by the end of the year. Share these goals with the department heads.

Phase 2—Department heads identify department goals needed to ensure that the organizational goals are met. This is the first level of alignment.

Phase 3—Department goals are given to managers to help them define the goals in their areas of responsibility with their groups or teams to meet the department goals.

Phase 4—Individual contributors work with their managers to determine goals for each area of responsibility in order to support their managers' goals and their department goals.

Let's see how the process of setting up goals plays out in this educational products and services company. In phase one, the business owner sets the strategic priority of increasing market share by 20 percent while maintaining a profit margin of 10 percent. Along with this priority, she sets these as strategic goals: (1) Increase market share by 20 percent; (2) maintain a margin of 10 percent. And she makes the commitment for these goals to be met by year end.

In phase two, operational goals are set. Remember, these are the goals that operationalize the strategic goals. They connect to the work in each department. The operational goals are as follows: (1) Meet monthly budget in terms of revenue and expenses; (2) maintain overall annual customer satisfaction at 80 percent.

In phase three, the operational or organization goals are broken down to departmental levels. The marketing manager committed to the following goals:

▪ Course participation at 98 percent to ensure that budgeted revenue is met.

▪ Customer satisfaction per course above 85 percent, to be measured after every course.

▪ Website traffic metrics, which is part of revenue pipeline.

▪ Meet or exceed monthly revenue targets. Maintain monthly expenses according to budget.

The communications manager committed to these goals:

▪ Increase newsletter recipient list by 20 per month.

▪ Maintain newsletter open rate of 30 percent.

▪ Distribute course-satisfaction findings within 24 hours of course.

▪ Call 100 percent of course participants one to two weeks prior to the date of the course to discuss prework and course objectives to ensure that all participants are ready for the course and not too advanced for it.

After each department manager commits to goals in collaboration with the other managers and interaction with the senior team, the managers carry out phase four by working with individuals in their departments to create supportive goals. Doing this together is a major factor in the success of setting and achieving goals.

While everyone will be involved at each level of the organization in establishing goals and plans, the depth of the involvement may differ. For example, the owner and the leadership team may collaborate in establishing the overall company goals and strategies. Managers and leadership may collaborate on operational plans for specific departments or units, and all employees would be involved in reviewing and providing feedback on the goals and the plans, especially as related to their responsibilities. This collaboration, sometimes called pipelining, is a key part of operational planning. *By sharing departmental operational plans with people in other areas of the company and by integrating plans, you ensure that you are not duplicating efforts and that you are on the same timelines and schedules for projects where there are interdependencies.* Throughout the process, you want everyone to be pipelining with each other as much as possible—talking, sharing meaningful information, and making sure that people aren't duplicating efforts, that they are working cross-functionally and synergistically, experimenting and discovering ways to do things better—aligning and optimizing efforts.

Organizing People and Areas of Responsibility

When structure is most effective, it arises from strategy. For example, at Iams, human resources managers sat at the top level of the organization chart, reflecting the importance that Iams placed on investing in and developing their people. Creating an organizational structure for achieving your goals that makes sense to people and reinforces your values and priorities is more meaningful than creating a structure that reflects the norm. You and your organization need to be agile and adaptable so that as priorities and goals change, you can serve them.

A great example of this showed up for a business owner. Through the strategic-planning process, it became obvious that the communications department was lagging in their use of technology to support the kinds of information and services that would be valued by their clients. Although they had seen this coming, they hadn't moved on it, and what had been an opportunity was now a weakness that was holding them back. The leadership team realized that they needed to invest in technology to serve their clients. This became a huge initiative for the IT department. In the past, IT had always been internally focused, and they were part of the operations department. The leadership team felt they needed to do something bold, so they moved the IT department into the client relations department, purposefully connecting IT to serve the clients. Although client relations is not a traditional place for IT, this reorganization made sense and it worked. The IT department still fulfilled its internal goals for the company while focusing 20 percent of its resources—people, money, projects, and time—on fulfilling their new goals, which created more value for their clients.

As you identify future goals, your organization will reflect those goals. For example, you may want to get into a new market, something you can see coming that you want to be well prepared for by advance research and study. You will want to begin exploring this long before you launch. You may hire one person, an expert—someone ideally suited to taking on this new opportunity—to explore, educate the leadership team, and propose how you might get into this market. As you expand your efforts and goals in this area, you may add people and other resources as well. Where is the best fit for this new group? Perhaps you want to expand into global operations. How would this area fit best into your organizational structure? You will have to determine how it most closely connects and is meaningful, based on goals, talent, responsibilities, and projects.

Retail organizations and service providers with online or physical locations may want to expand into the other arena. If you do this, where does this responsibility lie? In fast-growing organizations, understanding and clarifying areas of responsibility makes the transition easier when you are going from a few people who have numerous responsibilities to spreading the responsibilities out among many more people. It eliminates frustration and duplication and allows for collaboration. There are standard areas of responsibility like accounting, purchasing, and sales, but it may be beneficial to clarify these even more. You may want to differentiate prospective sales from current client sales.

Organizational structure is the process of organizing areas of responsibility and determining how much authority they have. Some organizations have a hierarchical, top-down structure. Others try to be as flat as possible, believing that this type of structure encourages initiative, higher-energy engagement, cross-functional collaboration, trust, innovation, transparency, and accountability.

Defining Jobs

Job descriptions are an important part of the structure of any business, and they are often overlooked, taken for granted. In fact, it's important that you write a job description for yourself and any partners so that your responsibilities are clear. It will be particularly useful as you shift more and more from day-to-day, hands-on business activity to stepping back for more strategic planning and letting others move in, take responsibility, and make decisions.

Probably the ideal way to create job descriptions is to sit down with employees and develop meaningful terms for their jobs, negotiating expectations and debating priorities as you go. This benefits everyone. Although you might not do this when you first hire someone (that might depend on the position you are hiring for), it is a good idea to routinely review job descriptions at least once per year—to sit down and ask, "What are you really doing?" Capture the reality by asking employees to be honest and clear about what their job entails. Make sure that these job-description reviews are a collaborative discussion of what is real right now and what is needed or expected for the future. Use these reviews to make sure that you are staying in touch with what is going on, listen and learn, and use the information to develop your perspective of the bigger picture.

When creating or revising job descriptions, keep in mind that objectives have to be measurable; all jobs have a purpose, and you have to create measuring sticks for every job. For some jobs, it is easier to make these objectives quantifiable, and for others it is harder. That's just part of the reality. Even when you are using qualitative standards, define them as precisely as you can, measuring them if possible. It's also important to limit job descriptions to no more than five responsibilities per job to clarify and focus purpose.

Publishing Your Organizational Structure

Sharing information is an underlying theme that runs through professional management. Publishing your organizational chart is consistent with that theme. It is useful for everyone in your organization, because it shows people who's running the show; who they report to; who's responsible for what; where they might find someone with the talent, skills, and expertise they need for a particular project; and how everyone's work connects. In a business with family members, the organizational chart is especially useful as a means of separating corporate and personal relationships.

The organizational chart tells managers and employees where they are in the big picture, perhaps where they've come from if they've come up through the ranks, where it's possible for them to progress, and who's there to help them. It clarifies lines of responsibility and potential opportunities for advancement. It also serves the important purpose of reinforcing people's sense of participation in the success of the company.

The owner of one business posts the organizational chart in the employee lunchroom, along with weekly profit-and-loss, safety, quality, and delivery-time reports. Employees know by 11 on Monday mornings whether the company was profitable the previous week and how well other goals were met. This business owner says that seeing the company's structure laid out so clearly has sparked conversations with employees about potential career paths and the training or credentials they would need to advance. Having everything out in the open makes it easier to keep employees on track.

Setting Up Performance Standards

Let's say that Kevin, a salesperson, knocks off work at 3 p.m. Do you assume that he is shirking his responsibilities and see it as a sign of poor performance? If so, you may be jumping to an incorrect conclusion because you've lost sight of what's really important. Hours worked is not the goal of any business; results are. If Kevin left at 3 but surpassed the performance of the other salespeople, who stopped at 6, you've got a worker who is not just performing well—he's exceeding expectations. Your job is to measure Kevin's results along with other salespeople's results. These measurements enable you to delegate work freely and see the progress you are making toward your future goals. You do this by using sales statistics and performance standards—just two examples of controls you can set in place. Failure to do this can have you failing to see the bigger picture with a more meaningful story. These performance-management tools or controls make it possible for you to have a very different, more appropriate kind of control.

Performance standards are the expectation bar for success in an area of responsibility. Standards describe the expectations. In customer service, a standard might be timeliness. How long does it take for a customer to receive a response? Quality might be another. How satisfied is the customer with the inquiry and the response?

When you are establishing standards for the first time, you might set baseline standards and then increase them by modest percentages, maybe 10 percent, in the next year. As you track and watch the trends, you will have more information on which to base realistic expectations. This process provides a sort of check against reality. Are the goals realistic? Do you need to reevaluate them and make adjustments? You want to use measurable, quantitative standards as much as possible. But some jobs lend themselves toward more qualitative criteria. In sales, for example, an employee can score herself based on dollars of sales completed, new business brought in, gross profit, or market share gained or lost. Other jobs require more thought. If you can't figure out what criteria to set for a particular job, ask the employee to help define good performance.

The owners of one business used to review employees on complex, subjective criteria, and there were no consequences for failing to meet objectives. As part of installing professional management, the owners developed standards for each job based on four primary metrics tied to sales, client retention, and profitability. Based on these metrics now in place, data is collected and shared with employees quarterly. To maintain a positive workplace culture and control how employees treat others, a fourth standard, a behavioral rating based on a 360-degree review, was implemented. The results of all these metrics are then tied to bonuses, so that the system can afford greater control and accountability.

Tessie and David, the co-owners of a home health-care company, reaped big rewards from a thoughtful overhaul of performance-based incentives and controls in their company that involved honing performance standards. After the overhaul, employees received weekly e-mails evaluating their performance as good, very good, or outstanding according to three standards. Quarterly bonuses—ranging from 10 percent to 25 percent of annual salaries—were based on these ratings.

Tessie and David worked with employees to specify targets for each job. As a result of these sessions, home health-care providers in the company were evaluated on quality-of-care measures; billing managers were evaluated on "days of sale outstanding," the average time elapsed between issuing a bill and collecting the money; even receptionists were rated on how quickly they answered incoming calls and the length of time callers were placed on hold. When the owners hit a roadblock trying to figure out performance standards for their IT director, they asked him for help and came up with a metric: the total length of time that systems were down during a quarter.

Several years after making the changes, employees have surpassed their initial performance targets many times, fueling controlled, healthy growth for the company. The system has also helped the company to win numerous workplace and customer-service awards.

The downside: the system triggered turnover at first. In a situation like this, superior performers can sometimes become pushy and overbearing. To counter bad behavior, Tessie and David recommend designing a "cultural and behavioral checkup" that discovers whether people are treating others with care, dignity, and respect. If employees flunk this checkup too many times, they're fired.

Performance standards and other controls you use to measure progress toward your goals need to be reviewed routinely. We will discuss performance reviews and other types of monitoring and review in chapter 7, where we explain metrics and monitoring as keys to accountability.

Reflective Review

- What difference might it make if you had a business model that you took the time to clearly define and clarify?

- Is your organization's structure determined by and in alignment with your strategic plan?

- Do you develop people in your organization to align with future growth? Or do you seek people with the experience and talent you need outside the organization to meet your needs for future growth?

- Do your people have a clear understanding of how the work in their area of responsibility connects to the work of others in different areas? Are people in different areas collaborating, working cross-functionally to optimize information sharing and understanding, and to support success in meeting goals?

- Do you have an up-to-date organizational chart? Have you shared it with employees? Is it in a location where it is easy for people to find it if they need to reference it?

- Are reporting lines clearly defined for every position in the organization, with no employee having more than one boss, no overlaps or duplications, and no gaps?

CHAPTER 7

THE KEYS TO ACCOUNTABILITY

erformance management is a process of setting up metrics and routines for measuring, monitoring, and reviewing information relevant to goals, and of examining that information against strategy, effort, and performance. This process is the basis of holding everyone accountable. It is most successful when you connect strategic goals to operational goals, operational goals to business results, and results to monitoring tools and a review process that helps you to see clearly where you stand in making progress toward your strategic goals. This is the most practical and meaningful way to plan for growth and account for everything and everyone that played a part in helping you to get there. *Performance management is the ongoing process of measuring, monitoring, and reviewing the structures you put in place to operationalize your goals.*

In this chapter, we'll explore how internal controls, key performance indicators, and a continuous improvement process can connect everything: your goals and every employee's contribution and performance in making progress toward meeting those goals. Your internal control process is a way to "control" results instead of people, to use practical metrics and tools for monitoring progress toward goals, to evaluate performance and examine strategy in light of results, and to connect everyone meaningfully. It is the operational check on everyone and everything going in the same direction, making progress toward your goals and ultimately toward your vision.

Regaining Control by Measuring and Monitoring Results

The greatest misconception about performance-management controls—metrics and reports—is that they take too much time, and they aren't valuable, which is why many business owners don't have them. Perhaps you think that your financial statements are all you need. Or maybe you just don't know what to measure, so you don't measure anything. However, setting up performance-management controls and a regular review process to accompany them is the way you ensure that strategic plans and goals are achieved. This is your *control process*. It is the way you ensure that every person at every level of the company is focused on achieving tangible, attainable goals—individually and collectively as teams, units, departments, and the organization—to achieve the larger strategic goals.

Controls, such as company policies, customer-satisfaction reports, sales, costs of services, and other key performance indicators, are necessary if you are going to make progress toward high-priority strategic goals. These tools and others like them benefit everyone.

- They tell you whether your business is heading in the right direction; they connect your strategy to your vision for the future, giving you a practical way to assess your progress.

- They give your employees information about where they stand and what to aim for, empowering them to do their best work.

- They prevent rude awakenings by keeping you on top of all aspects of your company.

- Most important, they free you up from micromanaging so that you can think about the future.

Controls are like a missile guidance system. Before a missile is even launched, the destination has been determined. In knowing the destination, the missile guidance system can be programmed to alert the missile when it begins to stray. You can aim for what you see as your business's final destination, but you need to have controls in place that will alert you when the business begins to go off course.

As companies grow and begin to exceed expectations, it's common for business owners to worry about losing their sense of control and competency. You want to know every detail of what's going on in the business at all times, on all fronts, which makes sense since this competency and control got you there in the first place. But when you try to control things by looking over the shoulders of your very competent employees and trying to govern their day-to-day activities, you're not doing your job and you're losing sight of the bigger picture.

To grow and be able to manage the growth, you and your entire organization benefit by your forecasting cash flow, controlling expenses, and setting production or performance standards—all examples of good business controls. These tools help you to see the growth coming, so that you can take steps to be prepared for it. Makes sense, doesn't it? You provide more of the kind of control that's helpful, and as a result, you get the information and learning you need, experience fewer surprises and less pressure, and can measure your progress. You know where you are.

The rise and fall of Nau, an outdoor-clothing company, illustrates the perils of not putting proper controls in place. Nau seemed to have everything going for it: a founder with startup experience, lots of marketing and technical talent, and a hefty $35 million in venture financing. But managers failed to set controls, which made it impossible to monitor key information on a regular basis and to hold anyone accountable. They paid a high premium for eco-friendly raw materials, donated 5 percent of revenue to nonprofits, built the payroll to 60 employees with full benefits, opened several costly retail stores, and then created numerous new product lines to fill them. After two years, Nau was headed straight off a cliff, hemorrhaging cash so badly that it was forced to seek out a white knight. A buyer acquired the company's trademarks and equipment for less than $5 million.[1]

Controls provide ongoing information about how far you've come, how your people and teams are performing, and how well your organization is progressing toward your objectives. Few business owners can let go of wanting to control as much as possible, micromanaging every little detail, until they understand how a system of controls works. Just like that missile guidance system, monitoring the right kinds of metrics will provide an early warning when a change in direction is needed.

Controls have extended benefits too. They send a message to customers, suppliers, distributors, lenders, and prospective employees that the business is run in a systematic, professional way. Ana, the founder of a business software company, says her employees cite business and financial controls as a selling point to prospective clients. Nobody wants to do business with a company that won't be around in a couple of years, and her company's controls ensure the establishment of an intentional process for measuring and monitoring goals, as well as a greater potential for growth. So, controls help you to regain control through a system of accountability, and they give you a firmer position in the marketplace.

Setting Up Controls—Measuring What Matters Most

Information that is meaningful to Ana's company is not necessarily most significant to you. It's best to take the time to identify the kind of data and metrics that are most valuable for you and the nature of your business. Ask yourself, "What information do we need to know on a consistent basis?" That's a great place to start.

When deciding what information will be most effective in helping guide your company and affording your employees self-control, it's usually best to stick to a total of five or six types of information. Trying to focus on too many may cause "analysis paralysis," or a feeling of being overwhelmed by too much data. If, for instance, you wanted to focus your business on all the potential business controls, you'd be back to micromanaging, but on a larger scale. Instead, it is more effective to be consistent and relentless in tracking the controls that are meaningful to your organization.

It makes a lot of sense that these measurements usually tie in with your strategic priority goals. You and your team will want to know if you are making progress and if you will meet your objectives. You may want to track metrics such as employee training, sales reports, speed of production and delivery, and customer satisfaction. I recommend tracking your most meaningful information monthly and making it easy for everyone in the organization to monitor that data, too. You will want to do the following:

- Develop and implement a system to capture the appropriate data.

- Leverage leading and lagging metrics that provide actionable insights.

- Be disciplined and committed to monitoring data over a period of time to get some real learning.

Three Types of Controls

Controls can be divided into three categories: preoperational, operational, and postoperational. Examples of each are in the table below.

Control System with Three Types of Controls

Preoperational	Operational	Postoperational
Strategic plan	Revenue data	Audits
Budget	Sales data	Sales reports
Hiring policies	Checkpoints	Performance reviews
Performance standards	Inspection	Budget reviews
Job descriptions	Production data	Strategic-planning progress review

Preoperational controls set guidelines and boundaries for future behavior. These are the controls that most small businesses commonly don't have in place because they don't know how to plan this way or because it is easy to get caught up in more exciting aspects of starting a business and ignore them. These controls include employment policies and handbooks; strategic, budget, production, or operating plans; a company structure that supports communication and accountability; job specifications and hiring processes; employee training and mentoring; job descriptions and performance standards.

Input from employees is crucial in establishing and developing these materials, and revisiting them periodically with employees will keep them effective and on target.

Operational controls provide oversight of current operations. They're your direct line to the office; you can call on the data in these monitoring tools to get the answer to "What's going on? How's it going?" instead of tapping on employees' shoulders or phoning incessantly. These controls include inspections; checkpoints; and real-time production, revenue, or sales data. These are most effective when employees have the power to act. At Iams, quality control was partly enforced by authorizing any employee or quality-control person to shut down the production line immediately if a problem with quality or cleanliness was detected. The line would remain idle until a quality inspector gave the green light to start up again.

Finally, *postoperational controls* report data and evidence about what was done in the past. These include financial reports and audits; reviews of progress against strategic, operating, or production plans; budget reviews; sales reports; and performance reviews.

One business owner likens his controls system to the vital signs that doctors monitor in their patients. Just as a physician tracks numerous indicators in a patient's blood, this business owner tracks 15 to 20 vital measures of his metal-fabricating business, including the following:

1. Sales	5. Sales by territory
2. Bookings to date	6. Ratios of deals closed to open quotes
3. Backlog	7. Costs to sales
4. New quotes	8. Payroll to sales

Taken together, these performance indicators constitute the main artery of his business. His system enables him to react to problems early, rather than waiting for an accountant's quarterly report to tell him the business is in trouble. For instance, controls provided an early warning a couple of years ago when prices for a key raw material started to skyrocket amid heavy buying by the Chinese, giving him time to ward off losses.

Sharing Information with Others— Successes and Mistakes

Information, from your vision and mission to your goals and current status, is so valuable to helping everyone work together and be successful that I recommend this three-point commitment: *share it, celebrate it, learn from it.* But sharing it can be hard for some people, and this often shows up in setting controls.

Setting controls—measuring, monitoring, and evaluating progress—requires a shift in mind-set and behavior for some business owners. Many are secretive about their business information. They don't want to share it. But it's important, even advantageous, that you share information with employees and that employees are continuously sharing information with you. This supports a collaborative process, one in which you and your workforce are contributing to a collage that represents the full story—the good news and the bad—of what is going on in your business.

There are various reasons for being secretive or private, but usually it is fear—that family members or friends will ask for a loan or a job; that employees will want a raise or will quit if they know the business is faltering; that professional advisors will raise their prices or that the union will want to negotiate a new contract. Whatever the reason, secrecy is rooted most commonly in fear.

Fear is not worthy of creating a barrier to achieving your goals. You don't want it to deter you from sharing information with others. People can't work effectively in the dark. No one likes surprises. Information sharing engages and empowers everyone in thinking about new ideas, solving problems, feeling part of the team and of something larger. It's important that everyone know what's really going on—that you be open and transparent with information—if you are going to hold people accountable and have a high-functioning culture in which everyone is helping each other to be successful. You can hold managers accountable for results only if they know in advance all the information about how their people are doing in time to adjust and improve their performance. When information about company goals, performance, and structures is shared, it allows employees to adjust accordingly.

Since sharing information with everyone is important, look for multiple ways to do it. You can post performance results on a variety of measures daily, hold quarterly employee meetings in each area of the business to review results, and schedule lunches with employee groups to discuss company or unit results or other concerns. This keeps everyone updated and on the same level.

In addition to reviewing vital information, I recommend celebrating it when it's appropriate and sharing it with everyone every month. One business displays its eight key strategic measurements in multiple places: in their staff lounge; online; in their biweekly newsletter; and in their president's letter that goes to their board each month. They use a color code to indicate the status of objectives:

■ Red indicates that the objective is in trouble and if the organization doesn't address it, they will likely not meet the year-end goal.

■ Yellow means that it is too close for comfort; the objective needs to be reviewed and watched closely.

■ Green makes everyone smile. The organization can rest easy that it is on track.

When one of their objectives showed yellow two months in a row, they called a meeting to assess the situation and to identify the issues and opportunities that needed to be addressed.

It's easy to share the successes and a lot harder to share the mistakes or failures. But there is so much to be gained by doing so. One business owner told me that his company considers it a high priority to learn from mistakes. To make sure that everyone is open to the process, they do not talk about motives, point fingers, or assign blame. They are on a learning mission; they want to understand why the mistake occurred and how they can prevent it from happening again. This business owner is skilled at asking questions, and he uses this skill to uncover the information they need: How did this happen? Why? What worked? What didn't work? What do we need to know? What did we miss? How can we improve our way of working on something like this? How can we prevent this kind of mistake from happening again? Finally, and this is very important, he asks, "Who else needs to know?"

Controls provide the current information, the reality checks, needed to be aware of how you are doing now and where you stand in relation to your long-term goal.

Without controls to reveal a company's current and potential growth, there is no guidance system, which leaves the business on a route with no touch points, no process for reexamining, adapting, and changing course. It's pretty much chaos—not even managed chaos. Controls help you to steer your business so that you can hit your target every time, or they can help you to understand why you missed it, and they provide everyone with the information needed to work together to solve problems, come up with innovative ideas, and be successful.

Setting Up Planned Time-Outs

One Aileron client has had great success managing risk and performance with what they call their "gate review." A gate review is an intentional, "temporary time-out" for the purpose of stopping momentum, slowing things down to measure outcomes, and assess outcomes in an effort to "eliminate catastrophic risk." Every application of the gate review process is a little different, depending on the level of risk in regard to time and money. For higher-risk investments, there are more gates, more questions, and more specific metrics. Lower-risk projects have fewer gates; they try to use a common-sense approach. This system provides an extremely effective structure for managing performance and accountability for projects in alignment with goals.

Optimizing Questions to Generate Information

There is no doubt in my mind that one of the most important tools for leading a professionally managed company is questions. Applying the skill of asking questions, learning to listen carefully to responses, taking as much time as you can in a given situation to deliberate, and using the information for decisions is what much of managing is about.

But business owners are very action oriented. The power of questions and deliberating is greatly underestimated. Most people want to jump right to an answer and take action. Most often the deeper, more valuable learning is in what emerges from a process of questioning and building what one business owner calls "collective knowledge."

Questions are power tools for unearthing the information you need. Ideally, you want everyone in your organization to be thinking in questions. The more everyone questions, challenges, digs deep for information, and lets one question lead to another and another, the more you increase your opportunities for reducing risk, solving problems, innovating, and ensuring that you are not making assumptions but seeing and understanding more . . . getting a greater, clearer perspective.

Research has shown that creating interruptions, like the planned time-outs and gate reviews implemented by the business owner mentioned earlier, produces better outcomes when these time-outs are used as opportunities to reevaluate the current plan, to gather all the current information, to assess if the plan is working, to question what you think you know and what you don't know, to be flexible and humble, and to challenge and to change course if needed. The researchers advise business leaders to use intentional interruptions to ask questions such as these: "What's the story now? Is it the same story as before? If not, how has it changed? And how, if at all, should we adjust our actions?" This sounds very reasonable, but in fact leaders tend to avoid changing plans once they are on a charted course, and they tend not to listen and take advice from others unless those people are perceived as experts.[2] Setting up a system of routine reviews is the most effective way to avoid runaway trains and to be more successful using the controls you have in place.

Learning to think in questions, to raise them continually, will help you see around corners and into the future. Use them freely, relentlessly, to deepen and extend your knowledge and to help others do the same. The practice of questioning and seeking more information keeps you open to other perspectives, an essential aspect of staying in touch with the present while planning for the future.

Questions you might use to generate metrics and tools for assessing performance and reviews follow. Note that some of these questions are meant to generate more questions. Others generate specific quantitative measures or as much detail as possible for qualitative ones.

- What do we consider a high-risk project?

- What do we know now? What kinds of information would help us to make a better decision? How can we get that information? Who can help us?

- What information do we need to know to assess this project and determine success?

- How would we identify it with specific quantitative criteria?

- How can we factually assess performance for a specific job, team, or project?

- What do we mean by quality?

■ What will success look like? How will we measure it?

■ What are potential roadblocks?

■ How are we performing?

Engaging in Routine Performance Reviews

Performance reviews play a significant part in the development of all employees. Any opportunity you have to sit face-to-face with your employees to talk and listen can be extremely valuable, and performance reviews are no exception. In fact, if they are conducted thoughtfully, they can prove to be important investments.

Since growing your talent is a high-priority value, and it is the manager's job to help employees grow, you will want to use the lion's share, as much as 80 percent, of your time during performance-review meetings to help employees explore career goals, to discuss training opportunities, and to coach or help them to find direction and processes for achieving their goals. During this time of exploration, ask the employee questions to find out as much as you can, so that together you can figure out some next steps and both of you feel that you are laying out a plan for the employee to move forward.

Performance reviews are a time for you to offer performance feedback to your employee, but they are also a time for them to give you feedback. Make sure that feedback goes two ways. Give employees an opportunity to critique their bosses, reviewing the performance and the level of support they provide to those employees.

People who are interested in taking on more responsibilities or in being on a management succession track appreciate knowing that there is a process with established standards for internal promotion or expansion of responsibilities. I recommend committing to at least 50 percent of your promotions from within. Using a five-point rating system (more than this is too complex), you can require vice presidents and other managers to review the performances of all salaried employees under their direct supervision every four or six months. Then you can meet annually with these managers to identify future successors to positions with expanded responsibilities.

Dealing with Low Performers

When you implement structural components, some people will like it and some people won't. If an employee resists or fights the implementation, it's appropriate to replace him. Sometimes low performers see the writing on the wall and leave, but either way, weeding out poor performers is part of the process. Employees at Iams who received poor results in their performance reviews were soon gone. We called it "pruning the tree," and we did it annually, which eliminated the need for massive restructuring every few years.

When a clearly communicated system of performance standards and reviews is utilized, there shouldn't be any question in the minds of low performers that they may need to leave. If these processes are effectively in place, employees will have plenty of advance notice that they aren't cutting it. Standards help take the emotion out of decision making.

That being said, it will always be difficult to fire some-one who can't meet the standards. You might employ people who have come through tough times with you, been dedicated, and given everything they could give, but their best just isn't enough. Those are the hardest ones to face. One business owner that Aileron has worked with has been stuck on this issue for a while. He has a loyal team that helped him grow the business to about 20 employees, but their skills aren't evolving with the business. His board and mentors have advised him to fire the veterans, but he can't bring himself to do so—even though he knows their presence is slowing the company's growth.

Sometimes it helps to assign a mentor to an underperforming employee or, if the person is at an executive level, to have one of your board members serve as a mentor. But if he can't cut it, you have to make the decision. You can't have a double standard; people either can perform or can't, and it's important that this control be in place and consistently applied. To be honest, many loyal long-timers are often aware that they aren't cutting it and may be relieved to be offered a severance package.

If you have to fire people, take part of the responsibility for it and find ways to help them get on with their lives. If employees have dedicated themselves to the organization, you owe it to them to help find them another spot in the company. If there isn't such a place, provide the resources necessary for them to find a suitable position elsewhere.

People can excel when they understand your expectations, but without direction, their performance will be unfocused and inconsistent. Performance reviews are a gesture of appreciation and respect; everybody is important, everybody gets one, and everybody is capable of fulfilling expectations with these in hand.

Structure with processes, standards, metrics, and reviews is a major way in which you embed practical, meaningful methods to develop the culture you want for your company. We will discuss this in the next chapter.

Reflective Review

- Which metrics do you look at on a routine basis? What do you learn? How do you use what you have learned to improve your business?

- What information would you like to know about your business? How often would you need to see this information updated to help you learn how to improve your business?

- What is most important to you? Quality? Customer satisfaction? How do you measure it? How do you learn from those metrics? How do you continuously improve in these most important areas?

- During performance reviews, are you actively listening and encouraging your employees to give you feedback?

- Have you clearly considered and communicated performance standards to all your employees?

CHAPTER 8

CULTURE—THE ENGINE MOVING YOUR BUSINESS

Ben wanted the value of continuous improvement and innovation to become embodied in every part of his company. He wanted everyone thinking about better ways to do things. To start the ball rolling, he decided that he would talk, one-on-one, with as many people in the company as he could. One day he met with a manufacturing manager, and another day he met with a janitor. He had a conversation with the person who was the last one on the line before the product went to the customer, and he talked to the customer-service representatives. Every day he talked to someone. During these conversations, he asked two questions: "What do we do well? What do we not do well?" Quickly, he realized that he learned more valuable information via the second question than the first. Jotting down notes as he listened, he made certain that after each conversation, he took action by initiating changes or at least exploring the issue, based on what he learned. When possible, he involved the employees and gave them the responsibility of holding him accountable. Pretty soon, the word around the organization was that the owner really cared what the employees thought. He really listened, and what people said mattered. They became eager to talk with him and to step forward with ideas.

Ben said that before this initiative, he sensed that many people didn't believe it was worth it to go out of their way to speak up or suggest anything. Things that people did notice or think of got discounted as unimportant and were swept aside. Ben wanted to capture everything, even the little things, but mostly he wanted everyone to develop the habit of bringing ideas for improvement forward. As a result of Ben's initiative, managers started having these conversations, too. They weren't told to do it; they just did it because they saw the positive impact and they wanted to be part of it. This voluntary participation by the managers had a significant effect on the overall cultural change. Pretty soon, individuals, teams, and departments were challenging themselves to come up with new ways to improve in all areas of the company, and the excitement around it was palpable.

Co-owners of a manufacturing company have intentionally created a flat rather than top-down organizational structure. They have scheduled hours for people to work, but they do not have a time-clock, punch-card mentality. "No one punches a clock. Everyone is treated like an adult." They have an honor system. People have keys, and they can flex their time. If they need to take off to go to a school program or take their child to the doctor, they use their own judgment and do it. There's no "hourly versus salary" attitude, either. The managers want everyone to be treated with respect. It's an important value in their company's culture, which they hope has a balance of high performance and high quality of life. They have very low employee turnover, so they must be doing something right.

My brief experience working for an American icon, General Motors, taught me how stifling a company's culture can be when not properly cultivated. When I landed my first job out of college as an accountant at General Motors (GM), spending 35 years at the same big company was thought to be a great career. It took me less than a month to figure out that a career at GM would be a disaster for me. Employees were treated like machines. You couldn't break the rules for the sake of innovation or cost savings. Even with a bona fide receiving ticket for items purchased, it still took six signatures to get an invoice paid.

I took the opposite tack at my own company, and I recommend that you do the same: set out to not only build a great company that makes great products or provides great services but *create a culture that inspires your employees to be the best they can be, and help them to become it.* You can't do that by setting onerous rules. You do it by establishing values and structure that support that goal, by leading and living that reality in everything you do, and by hiring the right people and empowering them to make good decisions. *It is your role to be the champion of your culture.* I often say that I wasn't the lion of Iams, I was just the roar.

In this chapter, we will explore what is involved in creating an intentional culture, one that is values based and makes your business an energizing place to be in while working to achieve your vision. In large part, it is intentionally placed structure, with processes, standards, metrics, and reviews, that turns ideals and values into real, practical, meaningful aspects of work life. But culture also derives from the way it *feels* to work at the company, because clear communication, or the lack of it, respectful behavior, a drive for excellence, a spirit of teamwork, the pace and pressure, the sense of freedom and of authority, a connection to a meaningful purpose, and more, really make a difference. Culture, a powerful discipline in the DOC, can clear the way and drive your company toward the goal, or it can put up a lot of unnecessary, damaging barriers.

Establishing an Intentional Culture

As part of the DOC, we define Culture as *an organization's ongoing process of fostering the environment, behaviors, and activities that bring the organization's beliefs and values to life.* By environment, we mean the tangible, physical environment, as well as the intangible—the feeling of what it's like to work in the organization and with the people.

Like structure, the culture of your company is going to develop whether you grow it intentionally or not. It's a lot better for everyone involved when you develop an intentional culture, one that is positive and highly functional; then it can be a source of real pride and positive energy.

Culture can go very deep, especially when the heritage, beliefs, and values of the organization are embodied. It is the thread that holds everyone together. Everything in a company has to be aligned not only strategically but also philosophically—some may even say spiritually. Culture says, "These are our beliefs and our values, and here is how we behave as a result. This is what we stand for." But before we can determine how we are going to show up and behave and where we are going to go, we have to figure out who we are. Culture is how all of those foundational underpinnings show up; they are the walk to your talk, the manifestation of your ideals and your values.

Identifying Your Values

In chapter 3, we talked about how a lack of self-awareness can hold your company back. You need to know yourself well—what you believe and what you value—in order to develop your vision, your mission, and the values of your organization. One of the biggest mistakes business owners make is not taking the time to figure that out. Knowing what matters most to you helps give you and your workforce a clear direction and understanding of what your company stands for. It helps you to clarify which projects are the highest priority and to determine the most valuable way you can spend your time. It brings everything into focus. Identifying your values brings your company into alignment with your structure, strategy, and vision because you can use them to align with your decisions, actions, interactions, and activities. Everyone plays a role, but you are the champion and you lead the way. All eyes are on you. As you hire and fire based on values, make decisions based on them, set standards, and live them in your every interaction, your employees, customers, vendors, bankers, and other stakeholders will see that you mean what you say—that you are aligning your values with your actions, decisions, and activities.

More than likely, if you are the founder, you can look at your personal values and see these reflected in the way your company operates and the type of people you have hired. If you value perfection or performance or humor, it's likely that these have become part of your culture. If you are not the founder, you may want to blend some of the values that are part of the company's history with those values that you feel are important right now, ones that you feel will create a culture where you want to work and others do, too.

Business owners are increasingly mindful of the power of a positive culture. One of the benefits is attracting better recruits. Gentle Giant, an East Coast moving company owned by Larry O'Toole, lures committed recruits by emphasizing fitness, training, and long-term career opportunities. In an industry where most companies can only find seasonal workers interested in short-term employment, this company attracts a higher caliber of worker partly because of aspects of the culture. For example, new hires run the steps of Harvard University's stadium to test their stamina. This generates a buzz that communicates the company's hard-driving work ethic and the value it places on personal challenge. Thanks in part to its culture, this company promotes most of its managers from within.[1]

Jim, a second-generation business owner, can't say enough about the difference between a culture that is meaningful and supportive in working toward your goals and one that is difficult and holds you back. For him, building a culture that had teamwork, great morale, and structure to help get things done made a world of difference. He described it this way: "We had a lot of individuals trying to work very hard instead of a team trying to come together and work smarter. For us, developing each of our skills, learning what each of us had to offer, and then working as a team as opposed to a bunch of individuals was a major accomplishment." Jim and his executive team learned to pull together, and one of their best moments was when they worked together to develop a mission, a vision, and core values for the company that were meaningful. "It is really what I see and what I want," Jim said.

Don't think that it's an easy process. Jim and his team did what a lot of people won't do. They tackled hard issues and had difficult conversations for the sake of intentionally building a better culture. That takes real courage. Jim said,

> There was so much tension and walls and frustration. We didn't even realize it. Either we ignored it or people just took their feeling home with them. We were literally crying and then hugging it out. I'm not exaggerating. I knew how important getting the culture right was when I came out of "The Course for Presidents." So, we worked very, very hard, and I feel that we are stronger than ever. We are accomplishing things that I'm incredibly happy about. My team and I are excited to go to work every day and to work together. It's amazing for the morale and the focus. People are able to look at a

plan and the steps that it takes to get to that accomplishment, and we do it. We check the list off, and it's done. When we look back at what we did, we are so impressed that we want to have more steps for growth and go toward more goals, and that is so exciting. We have really bright ideas and very exciting things that we are working on.

Jim and his team have put into place a performance system that includes quarterly goals, annual goals, and processes for holding everyone accountable. Laying out expectations has been a major factor in the company's ability to accomplish so much. And, he says, "people feel such satisfaction when they get their goals accomplished, and it is really very rewarding." On top of all that, Jim feels he has a much-improved quality of life—time with his family for coaching his son's baseball team, to go to games, and to take family vacations. Jim says that the change in his company's culture has made it possible for him to leave the business and know that everything is going to be fine.

A human resources manager told me that she learned a lot about establishing the value of continuous improvement and learning while getting her feet wet in her first job. Every three months, she met with her manager, and the manager would ask her: "What have you learned? What didn't make sense to you? Why do we do X or Y this way?" It didn't take long for her to start asking those questions of others and for her to start understanding the reason for them. She also discovered the positive energy that comes from being engaged in that mind-set.

Involving Others in Defining Values

Perhaps you aren't sure of two things: what you want your company's values to be and which ones are showing up now. You can bring this knowledge to the surface in many ways.

First, ask yourself, "What are my company values, or what do I want them to be?" If you haven't written them down, try to do so. If you are finding that your values aren't clear to you, talk to other people about the values they think are most important for a company. You might talk to peers, other business owners, employees, customers, your vendors, your banker, your accountant, and other advisors—anyone whose viewpoint you respect.

If you don't know what values are showing up, you will get clarity on that by having straightforward conversations with your employees, especially the ones who have been with you for a while. They may be eager to have this discussion. You can also clarify the values by evaluating the problems you are consistently having in your company, as well as the successes. You can ask your employees what they value about working for your company. They might say something like the following: being treated fairly, feeling respected, having opportunities to learn new things, having the freedom to be there if their family needs them without feeling guilty, opportunities to develop skills and grow into new areas. When you ask them what they don't like, you might learn about values that you had assumed were there but weren't clear to people. For example: not really knowing what is expected of them, not being clear about what you mean by doing their best and doing whatever it takes to get the job done, the feeling of being overwhelmed by the amount of work and the pressure to get it done.

You might do an analysis of your company's strengths and weaknesses. What do you think they are? What would other people say about this? Ask your customers, vendors, and employees, as well as members of the community. Is their feedback consistent with your perspective, and are the values showing up that you want representing your company?

You might want to know what work-environment characteristics your employees, your peers, and others admire. Which ones make them feel they are thriving? You might hear some of the following: honesty, attention to detail, work ethic, respect, collaboration, clear communication about expectations, having privacy and time to work on their own, working with people in other parts of the company and getting their perspective, opportunities to develop skills, permission to take some risk and develop new ideas.

When you consider these questions and get honest feedback from other people, what starts to emerge is a collage of values. You need to determine which ones align with your company values and which ones don't. Once you identify your values, you can then figure out how you can create structure and processes to put them in place so that they are clear and real and everyone is living them.

Making Decisions Based on
Values to Define Culture

Culture is one of your most powerful decision-making tools. It helps you decide which people to hire, to fire, or even to work with. You can use your values to determine which projects you will take and which customers you want to work with.

Selecting Customers

Think about the customers you really enjoy working with. More than likely, they share values with your organization. Now think of those customers you don't like working with. More than likely, you don't share similar values. One Aileron client believes so much in the power of values that he actively seeks out customers that share his company's values. His employees know this and really like to work there because they know that with shared values come good relationships, which make it an enjoyable place to work.

Hiring and Firing Employees

At Iams, we learned over time how to hire people who would enjoy working in our culture and would be motivated by it. While many companies focus on traditional résumé content, such as degrees or job experience, I'm a big believer in hiring for attitude and then training for skill.

When we did it the other way around—when we hired for skill and there wasn't a good culture fit—it usually caused a lot of grief. Too often, these people were corrosive influences. Even though many times they outperformed their peers, they were doing it in a way that didn't match the company culture, and they were causing a lot of damage in the process. This wreaks havoc internally and creates a nightmare for you to manage. It can drive away employees who are a good fit, those you want to hold on to. That's an unhealthy scenario.

In interviewing job candidates, we always probed to find out whether a person had integrity, common sense, and a love of hard work. At one point, though, we realized that we actually had people working for us who didn't like dogs and cats. When I asked why one salesman didn't like working dog shows, I was told, "Well, he hates dogs."

"How did he get into this company if he hates dogs?" I replied.

We soon began asking recruits about their attitudes toward pets. We also began using a values inventory, determining what values mattered most to them. This is a sensitive area; we didn't use it to stereotype people, make rigid judgments, or discriminate unfairly. It was just one of many resources we used to get to know people and foresee whether they would be a mutual fit.

For an employee to work well in a company, his values have to be compatible with those of the organization. One business owner sits down with new hires for what she calls "a beliefs interview." She talks with them about their personal and family background, and then describes the company's core beliefs, such as quality, trust, and caring for customers as if they were family. She offers recruits $1,000, no questions asked, to leave the company if, after starting work, they feel it isn't a good fit. She believes that it is worth the cost to find out early that an employee doesn't buy into the company's values, rather than down the road, after the employee has had a chance to damage the company's culture or reputation.

Another business owner pulls each new hire in for what he calls "45 minutes in the tank" with him. Alone in a conference room, this CEO delivers an explanation of his vision and the company's mission and impresses on the individual how critical each employee is to achieving both. He also explains the company's values, including commitment, reliability, integrity, and safety. New hires are invariably impressed, and one person even applauded when the CEO finished.

Left unmanaged, your culture can change and take on a false identity in which the values stated on the wall are different from the way the organization operates. If the culture isn't clarified, it is hard for others to hire to it, live to it, and help nurture it.

Dealing with Threats

As the leader of your organization and champion of your culture, you need to be aware of threats to the culture, from both inside and outside the company.

Sometimes, threats to the culture come from within. It's important to watch for internal conflicts between the values you claim to uphold and the priorities that guide day-to-day operations. At one company I worked for, managers professed high-quality standards, but the company's production quotas were so high that it was impossible to meet the quality standards without falling short of the quotas. Consequently, the quality manager spent most of his time watching the production manager, who devoted most of his time figuring out how to cheat the system. Nothing will undermine your company culture faster than that kind of internal inconsistency.

One tool for spotting internal conflicts is to run periodic employee surveys. One business owner asks his 100-plus employees every year to respond to a survey on how well the company is living up to its core values. He publishes the responses so that all employees can read about the issues that surface. If you use surveys to check the pulse of the organization and to get employee insight, make sure that you respect their time and their feedback by responding to it in a meaningful way. If you don't, you will lose credibility, and they will think that you don't really care about their issues.

Fueling Innovation

A high-functioning, positive culture can fuel innovation. Amy Simmons, owner of the ice-cream-parlor chain Amy's Ice Cream, hires her people for creativity and character, and then trains them in the company's history, values, and customer-service skills. New hires are taken on a secret shopping tour of competitors' stores. From then on, they're trusted to come up with the best ways to attract and entertain customers in their own particular stores, picking the background music and staging events. The culture has earned the company cult status in its Southern city—an advantage in competing with big, franchised chains.[2]

At Aileron, we strive to practice what we preach, to create the culture that exhibits the values we hold dear, to operate in alignment with our values and in the way we recommend you operate. We have a flat organization, in which employees add responsibilities and get increases based on performance. Different people have different responsibilities; all are valued. We use cross-functional teams when it makes sense for projects and especially for learning, to solve problems, or to improve processes so that we benefit from various perspectives.

Reflective Review

Take a little time right now to think about your company's values, the ones you see as the foundation of your business.

- Can you articulate these foundational values? Can you express them to others in a way that is understandable and meaningful?

- Are these values showing up in your internal and external environments?

- Do you need some structure and processes to make sure that they are showing up? In what areas do you need them?

- Are your values supporting your mission and vision? Are they creating a culture that you and others like working in and that is helping you and everyone else to feel excited about accomplishing goals?

CHAPTER 9

THE GIFT THAT
KEEPS ON GIVING

ew of you would turn me down if I offered you a resource that would help you to gain market share, improve profitability, and make better decisions. Yet among
the thousands of business owners I've met, mentored, or
addressed over the years, four out of five do just that when
they fail to set up an outside board.

If you ran a popcorn stand on the corner of Third and
Main in Dayton, Ohio, I would still suggest that you have
an outside board. By that, I don't mean a panel of family
members, paid advisors, or retirees; I mean a board made

up of executives you respect—impartial outsiders actively involved in the management of other companies at least as large as yours. If you're willing to work hard to make a board effective, and you're willing to subject yourself to scrutiny, it's the best investment you can make.

This chapter examines some common misconceptions about what effective boards in private enterprises do and don't do. It offers examples of the benefits these boards can bring in the form of better decision making and planning. It also shows why some issues are too complex or difficult to handle well without a board.

Why Bother with a Board?

Many business owners ask, "Why do I need an outside board?" Some believe that their company is unique; a board of outsiders wouldn't work for them and their company. Others rationalize that they already get enough advice from employees, family members, and paid advisors—their attorney, accountant, and banker. Frankly, they just don't think they need a board, can't see the purpose, and want to hold on to their autonomy. Perhaps you are among them, and you are thinking, "I can do anything I want; I own the company, and I like it that way." For a long time I thought that way, too. Nobody was going to tell me what to do in my own business!

That autonomy is exactly the reason why you need a board: a lack of analysis is a weakness in a privately held business. One of your board's most important functions is to strengthen your decision making by confronting you with opposing viewpoints to weigh. Every leader needs honest, objective feedback and someone to ask tough questions about plans, ideas, employees, and personal performance. Effective board members have nothing to gain or lose by telling you the truth. They are your sparring partners, people you can test your ideas with before you take those ideas into the marketplace. I always think that a good rule of thumb is to not buy anything that you can't sell. If you can't sell your plans and projects to an outside board, it's probably best not to implement them in your business either.

However, it's important to remember that the board isn't there to tell you what to do. This misconception springs from the public-company model, where a board may intervene in management to protect shareholder interests. This isn't the case in the privately owned enterprise. *A board for your company serves as a resource to help you with complex management and ownership issues. The goal is to discuss issues thoroughly, weigh all sides of a decision, and reach consensus.*

Business owners of private companies have one of the loneliest jobs in the world. Few family members, friends, employees, or paid advisors can truly understand what it's like to simultaneously play chief executive, owner, supervisor, spouse, parent, and citizen. Members of an outside board are uniquely able to understand these pressures.

Ultimately, the success of your board can be measured by your company's results:

- Did you gain market share?

- Did you improve profitability?

- Is the company better off today than it was last year?

- How do you feel about the quality of your leadership?

- Do you know where you want to take the business?

- Is your strategy clear, and are you headed in the right direction?

- Are your decisions thoughtful and sound?

- Do you have satisfactory succession and exit plans?

Role of the Board

Boards can help with several major leadership and management challenges, including clarifying your mission and vision, improving and executing your strategic plan, solving tough personnel problems, and figuring out succession plans.

Todd had long operated with the belief that his firm was king of the mountain. But after he held initial sessions with his board, members asked for more information about his vision. "I can't do anything for you if you don't tell me what you want to do with this business," one board member said. He returned with his vision: to be the leading contractor in his region. "OK, that's good," the same director replied. "Now tell me the size of the universe."

After doing some research, Todd was surprised to discover that his company held a far smaller share of the market than he thought. His board helped him restructure the company to achieve his vision, eliminating two less promising divisions and focusing on the part of the business that had more potential. Revenue nearly tripled over the next seven years, far outpacing growth in the overall market.

Another business owner, who's been meeting with his outside board for more than a decade, likens "the support to great coaching in football: you can watch all the game tapes in advance, scope out your competitors, and lay the best possible offensive and defensive plans, but when you hit the field, your strategy might not work." Just as a great coach helps with game-changing shifts at halftime, an effective board can help an embattled business owner respond and adapt to change in the marketplace.

He credits his board with helping him cut losses in preparation for the recession. Sales at his manufacturing company had tripled in the two years before the downturn but then hit a wall. He was procrastinating on cutbacks, but his board lit a fire under him, telling him to avoid burning up a lot of cash paying workers he wasn't going to need in a few months, when he would need the cash. He terminated his second shift and reduced the hours of his remaining workers. Orders soon plummeted to half prerecession levels. As unpleasant as those personnel decisions had been, it was better for him to keep the company as strong as possible and retain his most valued workers—the ones he wanted to stick around for the long haul.

In my own business, the tough questions raised by directors sparked some breakthroughs. Early in a period of rapid growth, one of my board members asked an important question that I couldn't answer: "Who buys your products?" This fundamental question caught me unprepared. I was amazed to discover that more than 70 percent of the people buying our products were women. This led us to ask some other questions and review some research on how women buyers made their product choices. We discovered that the color of the packaging mattered. We ran consumer panels to find out which colors they liked. When we went through an image makeover, those colors dominated our new packaging, which boosted sales—thanks to specific questions from my board.

Tough personnel decisions also can go better with the help of a board. One business owner recalled getting too involved in helping one new manager to succeed. The manager was falling short and had been for more than a year. But the business owner had invested so much in him, working with him and hoping he'd come around, that he couldn't cut him loose. He was too close to be objective, but his board had more distance, more perspective. Reviewing the manager's disappointing results, members pressed him to let the new manager go. Looking back, the business owner saw that it was the right decision.

Another entrepreneur said he had trouble firing loyal, longtime employees who couldn't perform. Pressure from his board helped him to see how much it was costing him. By spending valuable energy on underperformers, he was neglecting high-performing employees. Now that he understands the rewards of cutting the dead weight, he's better able to do this.

A board is uniquely qualified to help with the thorny problem of underperforming family members. It can evaluate the performance of family members employed in the business and help find solutions if any are underperforming.

You might get technical advice or help setting up wills, trusts, or stock transfers from a paid advisor or consultant, but only an outside board can spark the kind of tough-minded debate that forces you to consider alternatives in the context of your personal abilities, values, beliefs, and goals.

Imagine, for example, that you want to turn your business over to your children someday. You will need a succession plan. But this is one of many places where your inclinations as a parent—to bring your children into the business, to groom them, and to handpick those who receive management jobs—are likely to be bad for the business, and for your kids. You need a third party who can give an honest assessment of how capable your kids really are and who can support your decisions concerning their roles in your business. (In chapters 10 and 11 we discuss this further.)

Your board can walk you through this process, making sure that you confront the tough issues. In my experience, only board members can help with questions like these:

- Do you want to pass this business on?

- Do you want this business to survive you?

- If so, to whom should leadership and ownership be passed? How? When?

Board members can also be helpful in the event of your inability to work. You can share your wishes with the board and make sure that your family members meet the directors and have an opportunity to build trust in their competence and integrity, should something like that occur.

Your board serves you and your business best by sticking with big-picture issues. It is not the role of the board to be involved in solving day-to-day operating problems. That's the job of management. And although they may sometimes be helpful to staff members, board members do not take the place of your staff.

Selecting Board Members

My experience is that many business owners believe they won't be able to find good people who will want to serve on their boards. However, you may be amazed to discover that there are many qualified people who are willing and eager to serve. These people are in what I think of as the third stage in the cycle as business leaders.

As we cycle through our journey, we play three distinct roles. The first is *learning*. In this stage, we are soaking up as much knowledge as we can. *Doing* is the second stage, and during this stage, we are putting all that knowledge to use. In the third stage, *giving*, we are finally able to focus less energy and attention on ourselves, and we can help others. This is the time when we can share our knowledge, wisdom, and experience.

When you are forming an outside board, you are seeking help from those who are in the giving stage. These leaders experience joy in giving back, and they feel honored to help. Experienced managers enjoy serving on boards: suggesting solutions to problems; seeing the company try the ideas; and, ideally, watching those ideas work. They like being on the opposite side of the desk; they're honored that their opinions are valued, and very often they learn from the experience, too.

As you select board members, keep in mind that you are looking for risk-taking peers. This is very important. You want people that you respect, that are accomplished, and that you are willing to listen to. Neither you nor the board members can think of the other as subordinate. This relationship works best when you regard each other as peers.

Paying Your Board

Compensation for board members is based on your company's size, the number of meetings you anticipate, and the amount of effort you expect. You will want to set the fee at a level that recognizes the value of the board member's time, but not so high that it amounts to a major source of income.

Small companies, those doing about $30 million in sales, typically pay about $500 per board member per meeting (based on Aileron's experience). A survey we conducted showed that the average annual compensation for boards that met four times a year was $2,332. Other companies pay directors by the hour, basing the rate on what the owners pay themselves (assuming it isn't zero). It isn't wise to pay directors in stock, because owning a financial interest in your company risks blurring the objective viewpoint you need in a director.

It's advisable to set term limits, usually of no more than two to three years, with an optional extension to a maximum of five years. Most business owners set a 12-month period during which the new board member, the business owner, or the board as a whole can decide to end the relationship.

If your directors have taken you through a firestorm, it can be hard to cut off the relationship. Nevertheless, most directors have contributed all they have to offer after three to six years of service. The business will benefit from new players with a fresh perspective and the ability to focus on new goals. Board members who stay too long risk starting to think like insiders, depriving you of the rigor and objectivity you need.

Identifying Prospective Board Members

When you are ready to form a board, you will want to make a list of potential members. If you have included family members, your banker, competitors, customers, vendors, or paid advisors, I suggest crossing these people off your list. *Exclude anyone who has something to gain or lose by serving as a member of your board.* Paid advisors should already be giving you their best advice, so by filling your board with paid advisors, you lose the outsider's perspective that makes a board so valuable in the first place. Also, paid advisors may take advantage of their position to try to control you. I learned this when I made the classic mistake of having a paid advisor on my board. He recommended that the company do a real estate deal. We didn't do it, but we later learned that he would have benefited personally.

Guy, a business owner, made another classic mistake. He created a board that was too large. The ideal size for a board is three to five people. The size can vary, but it's best if the number doesn't exceed seven, to prevent board management and decision making from becoming unwieldy. Guy was inviting his friends and business associates to join his board until one of Aileron's advisors explained that his close personal ties with these people would prevent them from challenging him with the unpleasant truths or tough advice he needed to hear.

The point of the board is to give you access to talent you can't afford to hire. Go for the best and the brightest. Find experienced people who have already faced some of the challenges that lie ahead for you. Seek out executives who've run operations as big as or bigger than yours and who have complementary skill sets, especially in areas where you are weak. Look for people who can consistently provide fresh ideas and new thinking.

As you look for candidates, ask CEOs you know in your area for recommendations, and compile a list of CEOs, COOs, presidents, senior leaders, and divisional heads of companies within 100 miles. Then ask your business advisors, lawyers, and accountants for recommendations from the list. Your advisors should be able to make additional referrals, and I occasionally tapped a recruiter to help me find candidates.

Peers who are playing the game and have experience taking risks in business, just as you are, have much to offer. The owner of one fast-growing business-software firm recruited directors with experience in areas where she needed help. One is a veteran entrepreneur who has built and sold two successful companies in the industry; another, a retired industry executive, has the wisdom that this young business owner knows she needs; the third is a retired corporate chief financial officer with experience in mergers and initial public offerings. This board is well equipped to help the business owner through any challenge she may encounter.

Other business owners seek candidates in industries with similar demands. The owners of a privately held funeral home chain wanted a board familiar with the kinds of challenges they faced: running a capital- and labor-intensive business, maintaining a reputation for high-quality service, and operating multiple locations. To create a list of board candidates, the owners sought executives in the hospital, hotel, and airline industries—all service businesses with heavy capital and labor demands. They also invited restaurant and auto-dealership managers who managed multiple sites while maintaining a reputation for top-flight service.

Seek independent thinkers with the skills you need. If you are building a new manufacturing facility, search for a board member with experience in factory construction. Recruit people with high energy, prior board experience, and a genuine desire to serve. Recruit the best, not the best known. Look for the right talent for the right business issues for the right results.

Beyond these skills, you want to look for people you like, trust, and respect, and whose companies and management approaches you admire. You also want to recruit executives whose values are compatible with yours and who have compassion. When I recruited my board members, I made a point of visiting them at their businesses and watching how they treated subordinates. I highly recommend doing this. You learn a lot from the experience.

Recruiting Board Members

You will want to give yourself about six months to identify, screen, and meet candidates. (If you want to move faster, a consultant can help.) To lure top candidates, you will probably have to do some selling. You might put together an attractive portfolio that shows what you do and what you want to do in the future. If potential members can see a purpose, they'll be more likely to help.

Once you have a list of candidates, make time to have lunch with each one, and if the chemistry is right, invite the candidate to your company for a tour and introductions to your key people. Share product samples and information. Observe carefully. See if he is interested and enthusiastic.

If you agree on another meeting, visit the candidate's office. Tune in to the person's management style. Is a lot of time spent fighting fires? Or does he have two hours to speak with you? You have to trust your directors, respect them intellectually, and make sure they have integrity.

When the business-software entrepreneur mentioned earlier set her sights on recruiting a prominent financial executive to her board, he repeatedly refused, saying he was already too busy on numerous boards. But she pressed her case, taking the former CFO to lunch several times and wooing him with her long-term vision of giving back to the community. She laid out her idea of using her company's technological expertise to help regional food banks do a better job of distributing surplus perishables to the needy. Finally, after six months of saying no, the executive agreed to serve, and his presence on her board has been invaluable.

Managing Your Board

An outside board can be set up as either a board of directors or a board of advisors. Many business owners resist forming a board of directors because they fear losing control by empowering directors to vote, so most start with a board of advisors. While a board of directors is legally responsible to shareholders to vote on corporate matters, most boards in private businesses are more likely to reach consensus based on the collective wisdom of the group after a thorough discussion of issues. Votes tend to be unanimous. Directors serve at the pleasure of shareholders, reserving ultimate control for the business owner. Get some advice from your outside counsel in making a decision on what is best for you and your business.

Most boards meet quarterly for three or four hours at a time and hold special meetings when urgent issues arise. You will want to have board members who also expect to be available for occasional lunches or phone calls between meetings as needed.

Provide board members with meeting dates well in advance. Before the first meeting, send each director all the pertinent information she will need to help you with decision making, such as financial and operating statements, capital project information, reports on performance in key areas, and company newsletters. The faster you can educate new directors, the faster they can begin to help you.

After the first meeting, continue to send board packets at least two weeks in advance, including the latest financial information, an agenda, and other organizational updates. The person you designate as secretary to the board can help compile and send information—performance summaries, sales and budget, profit and sales per employee—as well as taking minutes at meetings and handling other organizational matters.

This preparation time can be one of the most valuable aspects of managing a board. One business owner says that preparing the board agenda and background materials every quarter forces him to be accountable and to think about the challenges ahead, the state of the organization, whether the right people are in the right jobs, and whether his client base is expanding according to plan. He says that in preparing for each new board session, he has to ask himself the critical question, "Are we doing the right things?"

Set up your agenda with the most important topics listed first. Some business owners assign a specific length of time to each topic, to control the length of the meeting and to make sure that essential issues are covered. Some also set aside time once a year to ask members for their suggestions on agenda topics for the future.

Only directors and the board secretary should attend meetings regularly. Top managers and advisors, even family members, can be invited as needed to make presentations, answer directors' questions, or get a better feel for the business for the future.

A board that is working well can often provide help between meetings. The owner of one 20-employee business says his chemistry with his three board members is so good that he can shoot them an e-mail between meetings and get thoughtful responses within the hour.

The Business Owner's Responsibilities

It takes courage to subject yourself to the review of a capable board, and it will be tough. If you're mentally exhausted afterward, you know it was a good meeting.

It isn't the board's job to criticize or confront you; rather, they are there to ask tough questions that nobody else has the courage to ask. A third-generation food business had as stockholders more than 60 members of the founding family, with an elderly second-generation patriarch serving as chairman. Although sales were more than $250 million, only a paltry 1 percent of that was reaching the bottom line.

Two cousins with management roles and a controlling interest set up an outside board with help from a consultant. The directors were able to help the company move toward resolving some long-standing problems. For example, the chairman loved using company-owned trucks for distribution, a costly pet project that was draining cash and distracting management from pressing problems. No one in the family or in management could persuade the chairman to sell his beloved trucks and use cheaper commercial trucking lines.

But when outside board members, who had nothing to gain or lose personally, took on the patriarch, he eventually relented. After five years, they had cut costs, fielded profitable new products, and tapped new regional markets, which helped double sales and multiply profit 20-fold.

Part of a board's job is to assess your performance. A leader needs honest feedback, no matter how hard it is to take. You can't see the world clearly from your own little cocoon. My board worked hard to help me be successful, but they also held me accountable and tried to keep me out of trouble. Your board will help you do the same.

The single most important role you can play when working with your board is that of a knowledge seeker. You and your company will benefit from the knowledge, perspective, insight, and experience of your board members. Your responsibility is to listen with an openness and willingness to learn, taking in the advice of those you respect and trust. This can be challenging for leaders, who are accustomed to having the answers, but it is a valuable shift—essential if you truly want your company to grow. Your commitment to listening, as opposed to driving your own personal agenda, is vital.

You also will want to be mindful of not trying to sell the board on your opinions, controlling the discussion, or dictating direction. You can accomplish this by establishing an understanding that you and the board members have a collegial, peer relationship, not a hierarchical one. Your agendas, meeting style, and tone will support this mutually respectful relationship. This will encourage the flow of opinions and ideas, and it will foster creativity. It will also make the tough discussions easier to have.

It is important to focus on major issues with the board. A good rule of thumb is to spend 80 percent of your time on discussions of current and forward-looking issues and only 20 percent of your time on issues that happened in the past. Focus on the make-or-break goals: the ends to be achieved.

The Board Members' Responsibilities

When board members accept a position on your board, they also take on some responsibilities, for which they will want to hold each other accountable. All of these responsibilities ensure that you will have a high-functioning board, which is just what you want.

Board members will want to make sure that everyone is participating. You will want to be aware of each member's preparation and participation. Have they reviewed the information you sent in advance of each session? This is important so that they can be effective as a group, with each member fully contributing.

Each board member needs to adopt an attitude of representing the ownership of the company, with loyalty to the owner of the company, not the company itself. The board members are not a part of the organization, and it is important that they understand this. Their own personal agendas cannot have any influence on their board-level opinions and advice.

It is important that the board become a cohesive group and that the members feel a responsibility to the group. Board decisions are made collectively as one voice. Members need to hold each other accountable to make sure that the board is doing the best job possible. If someone is falling short of expectations, other members have a responsibility to intervene and correct the problem.

One business owner, who was very new to working with a board, was concerned because one of his board members, someone less experienced as a board member, wasn't coming to meetings well prepared. This was important to the business owner; he wanted each member of his board to challenge him and to push him hard, so he solicited the help of a more experienced member of his board. They agreed that an appropriate approach would be for the more experienced board member to confront the less experienced one privately. During a break in their next board meeting, the more experienced board member had a private conversation with his less experienced and less prepared colleague. Although the business owner was not involved in the conversation, he was aware of it. This was all that was needed to resolve the problem. In the following board meetings, all members came prepared and ready to challenge the business owner in respectful, productive, and valuable ways, and he was very grateful to the more experienced board member for his help.

Although the board's decisions are collective, it's important that before those decisions are made, differing viewpoints have been heard. Everyone needs to encourage diverse opinions, listening to them, questioning and maybe challenging them, but never stifling them or sweeping them under the carpet. Consensus emerges in the final decision, which will be far more valuable when all perspectives are heard.

The role of the board is to be focused on the future, the direction and positioning of the company—only the issues that affect your organization's long-term direction and success. I call this *thinking outward and forward*, as opposed to inward and backward. The board can serve best by focusing on the external factors that could affect the organization. The members' perspective and analysis of those issues can be critical for the owner. And it is crucial that the board work on the right agenda.

Once all board members express their opinions, it's important for them to reach a decision that is in the best interest of the company. When a final decision has been made, all members need to support it.

The board really does become your resource for getting honest advice, for holding you accountable, and for keeping you focused. One business owner tells a story of how during a board meeting, as they tackled the agenda, his board members sensed that the business owner's mind was elsewhere or there was something he wasn't telling them. Finally, one board member spoke up: "Tom, what is going on? You seem distracted and on edge." Tom explained that he had had a big argument with his wife that morning over something insignificant; it just blew out of proportion. He apologized for letting it interfere with the meeting. Instead of moving on, the board members asked Tom if he would share the situation with them. Tom told them that his wife had been complaining about their gravel driveway ruining her shoes. This was an ongoing sore point at home. The board told Tom, "Pave your driveway. You have the money. It is important to you and your family to resolve this chronic issue. You will be happier, and so will your team. Think about it. How often does this issue come up and affect your attitude at work?" Tom had never thought this would be the type of issue that his board would help him resolve. But it took his board to help him see how this issue and his inaction about it was affecting him, his wife, his family life, and his work life. Their questions made him realize that it was a bigger, more important issue than he had realized.

Breaking the Ice with a Mock Board Meeting

Many business owners who have never worked with a board can't imagine the value until they experience it. I can understand this. All the work can be overwhelming, and involving others in your biggest decisions can feel intimidating. If you have concerns like this, a great way to get the experience without making the full commitment is to set up a mock board meeting. It is a chance for you to practice and see the value. At Aileron, we frequently help business owners to set up this one-time meeting to reduce whatever barriers may be holding them back. While the business owner prepares for the meeting, Aileron finds appropriate people to form the board and sets up the meeting. This might be something that you would like to consider.

Reflective Review

- ▪ What is holding you back from creating a board of advisors?

- ▪ What goal do you have that could more likely be attained if you had a board with specific expertise and experience? Can you think of anyone with that expertise and experience who might serve on your board?

- ▪ What questions might you ask yourself in preparation for a board meeting? How would routinely preparing for a board meeting help you?

- ▪ Which of your colleagues or friends do you call when you need to talk through an issue? Do you know someone you think of as totally objective, someone who is willing to listen and ask questions to help you?

PART THREE
LIVING PROFESSIONAL MANAGEMENT

CHAPTER 10

THE BUSINESS OF
THE FAMILY

I believe it is imperative to invest as much care in the business of the family as you do in the family business. What does that mean? I think it means acknowledging that your business has an impact on your family and purposefully managing that impact, proactively determining how the family will be involved. In this chapter, we will look at some of the more common issues.

Living Professional Management at Home

When you put your capital at risk to grow your business, your family has a stake in that risk, too. Everyone will be affected by long workdays or time spent away, by worries and accomplishments, by all the changes that growth brings. In their own way, whether or not they are employees of your business, your family members play an important role. They do their jobs so that you can do your job. It's all part of having a whole, authentic, and balanced life.

Just as you don't walk out your door for work and leave your family behind, you don't come home and leave work completely behind. Although some business owners try to do so, you don't have to split your life in half. You can consciously connect all parts of yourself—your family and your business—and find a good balance. Share this part of yourself with your family, but do it consciously. Look at the bigger picture, get perspective, and incorporate your values. Partner with your spouse, and talk to your children as appropriate; share with them, and let them know you—all of you, not just certain parts. And if necessary, bring in expert advisors to help you. As a result, you will have more meaningful relationships with your family members.

You will acquire new skills as you learn and live professional management in your business. It's amazing how much the knowledge and skills you learn apply at home too. Take them home, and use them in all areas of your life. Planning your life is probably more important than planning for your business; however, many people don't put forth the same effort.

I did not start out conscious of how my choices and behaviors affected my family. I made a lot of mistakes along the way, and to be honest, I have regrets. The good news is that I've learned—from my own experience, from my children, my wife, and experts—that there are common but avoidable negative impacts. By being proactive, you can create more positive impacts and more learning for everyone.

Creating Your Vision

If dreaming, thinking about your vision, and turning it into reality is important in your business, it is certainly just as important in your family. Why not have a family dream journal so that everyone can practice thinking about and expressing their hopes and dreams for the family. You will want everyone to value the practice of thinking about and writing down their heartfelt dreams, so it will be important for you to participate. You might want to establish a time for sharing and talking about what is in the journal, what you might do as a family to make those dreams realities. How might you turn them into a vision for the family? Perhaps you do this on a regular basis. Maybe the dream journal can become part of a holiday, anniversary, or birthday tradition. You and your family can decide how to make this aspect of your lives inspiring, practical, and meaningful to you.

Think about and write down your values too. What is most important to you? How do you want your values to show up in your family life? Encourage questions and conversations with your children. Make conscious choices around what is important to you—what you do, how you spend time and money, how you treat people—so that you make the connection between what you say is important and what you do. Just as you do for your business, re-visit your values once or twice a year to recommit to them, change them, or refine them.

Avoid Making Assumptions

Hopefully, the business you are building reflects your personal dream, values, and desires. And, hopefully, you are also sharing all parts of that with your family members, especially if your dream and desires include them. A common problem that arises in families is a lack of communication by the business owner. Instead, the business owner makes assumptions and formulates expectations without giving everyone involved a chance to weigh in. It's a good idea to consider some important questions: Do you expect your kids to follow in your footsteps? Are you assuming that this is what they will do? Or do you encourage them to pursue their own dreams? For everyone concerned, it's important to keep the lines of communication open. Don't make assumptions yourself, and don't allow your kids to make assumptions about what you expect. Talk to them about their options, their dreams, and their desires. Make sure that everyone is clear, or at least that the lines of communication are open for questions, explorations, and maybe different decisions.

Making and Keeping Commitments

At your business, you manage your schedule carefully and with commitment. Once you make a commitment to a meeting or event, you are not likely to miss it, because it is important to you. It has value. Hold yourself to the same standard at home. It's all part of walking the talk, and if you've told your child that you will be at a soccer game or a band concert, it's important that you keep your word and show up.

Looking back, I wish I hadn't missed so many of my children's activities. Some of the kids later told me that they wished the same thing. Were I to start again, I'd look more often at our family calendar and block out time in my own schedule for family, just as I did for business meetings. It's important to prioritize and schedule family time and respect the demands of your home life as you do with your business. It's too easy to neglect your personal life when you're consumed with your work.

Tony, the leader of an engineering company, places a high value on family. It is so important to him that it is a company value too. During the summer after his son, Wade, was going to graduate from high school, Tony wanted to take a two-month cycling trip with him. This was important to Tony, and because he had built a culture that valued this choice and because he trusted his management team, he felt that he could leave the business and rely on them, as well as everyone else. He made it clear that he would be available by e-mail and phone; he wasn't abandoning everyone.

However, Tony's management team understood the significance of this cycling trip for him and his son. They really stepped up, letting everyone know that while Tony was away, he was to receive no phone calls, no e-mails. They could and would handle anything that came their way. Tony had the full support of his company so that he could have this once-in-a-lifetime experience with his son. It turned out to be a highly valuable experience for everyone, and it was a great way for Tony to live by example this high-priority value in his life.

Sharing the Good, the Bad, and the Ugly

You have the best of intentions, but you may not always be honest with your family about situations in the business or mistakes you have made. Talking about these issues at the dinner table and letting your children hear about your experiences can be wonderful learning opportunities for them. These opportunities show your family that you are human, that you make mistakes. Sharing like this gives them a chance to offer opinions and support, and gives all of you the opportunity to build trust through listening to and respecting each other. You are also showing everyone that vulnerability is a strength, not a weakness.

I probably erred in the opposite direction. Talking with my family, I made a point of avoiding the downside of my workdays. In my own mind, I was protecting them, but my children say that they would like to have heard more about my failures. My son Tim says I made making money look easy. My daughter Tina recalls being surprised as an adult when she overheard me tell an advisor that some of my decisions had misfired. According to my daughter Cate, who knows this issue as both a child of and a spouse of a business owner, *your challenge is to communicate openly and stay connected emotionally, without conveying a lot of fear and anxiety to the family*. Children benefit, she says, from seeing their parents talk openly about day-to-day feelings, doubts, fears, and challenges. My son Mike makes a point of talking to his children about his opportunities, the areas where he could have done better, the failures he experienced, and how he felt about it all. And while he includes "the good, the bad, and the ugly," he says, "I tell them that just because you fear something, it doesn't mean you can't continue to move through it."

It is important for you to make conscious decisions about the information you share with your family about the business. It's more considerate and respectful to everyone not to let conversations about your business dominate at the dinner table but to be real; your business is a big part of your life, and it's appropriate that you share your experiences and your concerns. You will want to be sensitive to finding a balance.

By the same token, you want to show genuine interest in how everyone else has spent their day and what is on their minds. You want to really listen to them, ask questions, and listen some more as they talk about their activities and relationships. Sometimes you will want to talk about what's going on at work. Just make sure that you think about it first. Don't unload a whole pile of stresses upon your family; be discerning. When you communicate about the business, be honest and balanced about the information you provide.

Be aware that your children are constantly picking up attitudes and beliefs about the business based on your words and the example you set. Without realizing it, you can sometimes pass on negative attitudes. If you focus only on the stress and don't share the positives, your children may resent the business for making you miserable. On the other hand, if you talk only about your victories, they will think it's easy. Your success could be intimidating, making it hard for anyone else to try to fill your shoes. Share news and concerns, but share the excitement of some of the hard-earned triumphs too. When you do bring up business issues, look around and try to pick up on any questions that people have. Encourage conversation so that everyone can learn something.

Learning How to Wear Many Hats

As family member and business owner, you have many roles. A challenge you'll face is learning how to shift from one role to the next: business owner, maybe CEO or president, shareholder, parent, family banker, and spouse. Jumping among these roles can complicate family communication. If you are a CEO/business leader all day, making executive decisions, it can be hard to turn that off when you go home at night. But it's important; your family needs you to be a spouse and a parent. Your role needs to shift at home, and you have to be mindful of which hat others expect you to be wearing at any given moment.

Working with a family business consultant, our family used the idea of "changing hats" to improve communication. We even had different hats made, labeling them with our various roles, such as "Father" or "Business Owner" to remind me and others of my role at that moment. My son Tim says that several years ago he asked me for advice on a matter. My response, according to Tim, was: "That is the stupidest idea I ever heard." "Which hat are you wearing now?" Tim asked. "Business owner," I said. "Well, take off that one and put on your father hat," Tim replied. We had the hats nearby, so I actually did that. And in the mind-set of a father, Tim says, I gave him a more measured response.

As my son, a business owner, a spouse, and a father himself, Tim understands this challenge from multiple points of view. "To the business owner," he says, "everything in the business is mission critical. But to the kid, it's not. The children don't really care how much money you have. The kid feels, 'Dad, I don't want you to fix anything.

I just want you to listen.' What the kid wants you to do is, 'Sit, feel, and talk. Sit, feel, and talk.' But the entrepreneur is all about, 'Fix it, move. Fix it, move.' He doesn't know how to shut that down and just listen."

Offering Work Experience to Your Children

Many business owners ask me if they should allow their children to work in their companies. In children's early years while they are in school, I think they need to develop their own work ethic. This can be accomplished in a lot of different ways. I always allowed my kids to work at Iams during school breaks and in part-time positions during the school year. They were assigned real responsibilities and a manager who was expected to hold them accountable and develop them, just like any other employee. My kids worked in product packaging. They cleaned the plant, worked on inventory audits, and did many other necessary but low-level jobs. I never gave them a position that they were not qualified to fill. I felt that they had to earn their increases in responsibility.

When the owner's kids are in the workplace, it can create unnecessary turmoil if expectations are not clearly communicated. If you expect your child to be treated with deference or as special in some way, then you need to communicate this to everyone—the employees and your child. I highly recommend that you set the expectation that your child is to be treated like every other employee. To do this, you must be committed. If you allow special treatment, it will only confuse people.

Showing Appreciation

If I could go back, I would have listened and given more of my attention to my wife, Mary. I would have thanked her more often for her support and for raising our children.

Your family supports you in everything you do; take care in showing them how much you appreciate their support. Communicate this effectively and repeatedly. Make sure that you stay connected emotionally, and genuinely listen and engage in conversations.

Working with Your Spouse

In this chapter, I've tried to highlight the nuances and complexities that owning a business can have for a family. It seems to me that being aware of them and intentionally facing them can make a real difference in your family's experience. This is especially true if you and your spouse work together in your business. It can be wonderful to build your business together and to run your household and raise your children. But it can also be a big challenge. The hat scenario described earlier takes on even greater meaning. It's probably twice as important for you and your spouse to talk about and agree on roles and responsibilities, to define your job descriptions and performance standards, and to make conscious choices around the focus at home and the boundaries of your conversations. Serena and Steve said that after implementing professional management in their company and understanding how it could work at home, they were able to live two dreams: having a successful business and having time for their family.

Reflective Review

■ How will decisions be made about the business with the family? What will you and your spouse determine jointly? Independently? What decisions will be made by the whole family?

■ What will you share about the business at home? How will you make sure that you balance the struggles with the learning, the challenges with the achievements?

■ What information and how much will you want to share with others outside the family? How will you talk to your spouse and children about this and set up some boundaries?

CHAPTER 11

SUSTAINABILITY AND SUCCESSION

Since planning and setting direction for the future is integral to professional management, succession planning and sustainability are a natural part of it. But it is common for business owners who are otherwise capable planners—who produce forward-looking vision and mission statements, create bold strategic plans, and do a good job of scanning the horizon for change—to fall short in this area: they run their companies as if they're never going to retire. Many business owners avoid rather than address this crucial responsibility.

Have you thought about an exit plan for yourself? Do you want the business to stay in the family, and if so, do you want to pass on management of the business, ownership, or both? If not, what prospects do you see for management and ownership? What happens to the business if something happens to you and you can't run it anymore?

I didn't know the answers to these questions when I was building my business. Not many business owners do. But if you don't figure out the answers yourself, someone else will do it for you. If the business owner "does not have the courage to face the problems of the future, then his banker and attorney will do it for him on the way back from his funeral—four cars back from the flowers," Leon Danco says.[1]

This chapter provides insights on planning for a successful transition that supports the long-term sustainability of your company. I hope that this chapter will motivate even young business owners to think about a succession plan in case of an emergency—an exit plan that is by choice—and how they would like their business to live on. If your business started with a dream, it can end as part of the fulfillment of a dream, too.

Considerations for Succession Planning

Few entrepreneurs plan for succession, which may be why so few family businesses pass successfully from one generation to the next. Family discord, or the fear of it, is a common obstacle. This can take many forms: brothers and sisters who don't get along; other family members who risk destroying the company by fighting among themselves; employees who are ready to revolt because the family can't reach an agreement on what direction to take the business; or second- or third-generation owners who spend all the money and bleed the company dry.

These situations fuel a damaging stereotype: that family business owners aren't in the game for the long haul.

This perception undermines business relationships with all kinds of important stakeholders, from employees and business partners to suppliers, distributors, and lenders.

Every business has the potential to survive for generations. To support this potential, you will want to reach out for expert help in shaping a succession plan and building an exit plan.

The long-term health of the enterprise is the highest priority because it is in everyone's best interest, even if some of the people involved can't see that. Peter Drucker wrote that "both the business and the family will survive and do well only if the family serves the business. Neither will do well if the business is run to serve the family."[2]

It is wise to begin planning early, so that you can shape the expectations of all involved, from managers and employees to spouses and children. This requires tackling some tough questions, such as, are your family members the right people to lead the business into the future? The best thing for the business might be to look outside for the leadership and management skills you need. Peg and Mark, first-generation business owners, were delighted that their son wanted to take over the company, and after careful consideration everyone agreed that this would be a great choice for the company. Peg wanted to transition out of the business earlier than her husband because she wanted to be able to focus her time and energy on helping her parents as they aged and needed more help. It turned out that her timing was just about perfect. Her parents did have health issues, and she wanted to be there for them. She was so appreciative that they had a plan in place, which made for a much smoother transition.

Having a succession plan and exit strategy is a part of your responsibility; it is a part of your accountability; and it is the thoughtful, responsible, respectful thing to do. I think of it as part of the business owner's role as the long-term thinker/visionary of the company; it's a big piece of long-term planning for your business.

Developing a Structure and Getting Advice

If you want your business to survive as a family enterprise, you have to design a structure to serve that goal. Too often, business owners get all of their advice from lawyers or tax accountants. These advisors are intent on the most tax-effective way to transition a business. They can help you to reach that goal, but the most tax-effective route isn't always best for the family, the business, or the next generation.

Your outside board is the best resource for taking a broader approach to planning. Unlike everyone else involved, your board members have nothing to gain or lose from your succession decisions. You need their experience. They can provide an honest assessment of the capabilities of your children or other potential successors, the preparations required for leadership, and a strategy for passing the baton in a way that confers both the responsibilities and the privileges of leadership.

Being Realistic about Family Members as Successors

It is most practical to be thoughtful about bringing your children or other relatives into the business. If a family member wants to work for you, think carefully before you say yes.

Once he or she is employed, it can be difficult to end that relationship.

On the other hand, don't simply assume that your children want to work in the family business. Sometimes, joining the family business is their dream; other times, they may decide that it's your dream, not theirs.

The son of one business founder says he felt so pressured to join his father's company that as a senior in college, he dropped his own job-hunting plans and agreed out of loyalty to interview with his father's head of sales. The son didn't love the business, but he loved the man who ran it. Not surprisingly, he didn't last long at the company; he left after two years for another job, and the company was eventually sold.[3]

If you decide to allow your children to enter the business, family-business consultant and author John L. Ward recommends that you make them feel welcome but don't pressure them. Set some rules about how and when a child can join the business, communicate these guidelines early, and enforce them fairly.

It's more beneficial to everyone when all successors have gained outside experience. When family members do enter the business, they should take a job that the organization clearly needs filled—one that they are qualified for. And finally, entering family members should each be assigned a mentor (who is not a parent) to guide, teach, and evaluate their performance.[4]

If you want members of the younger generation to manage the business, you need to think about whether or not you are willing to invest the time and money needed to prepare them to take over. This is an important determinant in helping them and the company to succeed in the short term and in the long term.

Having Some Skin in the Game

One of the biggest mistakes I see among business owners is that they make it too easy for their adult children to take over the business. The founder of a machine-tool business passed ownership to his sons upon his death. Several years later, one of the sons came to me and asked me to invest in the company. I asked him if he had exhausted his bank credit lines. He said the bank wanted to put a lien on his and his sibling's houses, and he and his brother thought taking out a second mortgage was asking too much.

"Are you kidding me?" I said. I nearly lost my house in my early days, betting on my company's future. Other entrepreneurs max out student loans and hock their wedding gifts to keep their businesses going. My advice to this second-generation business owner was to not come back to me until he and his brother had pledged every personal asset they could to the business.

Successors should have some skin in the game. Business owners should not simply give the business to their kids; they should sell it to them. My advice is to have your children buy the company; take preferred stock, a note, or subordinated debt from them before allowing them to run it. Good financial advisors and consultants can help.

This approach can help kindle an entrepreneurial spark in successor generations. Some business-owning families have managed to keep this spark for decades. One family earned its original fortune in milling and manufacturing and has now been in business for seven generations in many different ways, including creating other successful businesses, such as several forest-products companies and a wealth management firm.[5]

Getting Outside Experience

Many business owners bring their kids into the business during or straight out of school because they want them to see how Mom or Dad does things, but this is often a mistake.

A contractor who once built a new house for Mary and me had two sons that he wanted to eventually hand the business to. One was a tradesman and the other was a college student. I asked where they were working, and he told me they were already working in the business. "I want them to know how I do things," he said. The problem was, his sons already knew how he did things. What they needed was to get away and learn how other people ran a business so that they could make their own critical, independent judgments. Children won't ever really learn as long as Mom or Dad is calling the shots.

Working elsewhere gives adult children a chance to make mistakes and learn from them, away from the watchful eyes of their parents and on an equal footing with co-workers, free of the stigma of being "the boss's kid." It also gives them the opportunity to gain confidence and maturity through their own experience, to make their own mark, and to get off to a strong start when they return to the family business.

Nick Horman Jr., a self-described "third-generation pickler" who worked at his father's food company, chafed under his dad's rule, seeing him more as a father than as a boss. The two fought during the son's teenage years, and the fighting resumed when he returned to the family business after college. Nick Jr. eventually left to follow his own interests but returned after two years, wiser and more mature, and he launched the company's first retail product line. With his outside experience, he had learned to appreciate his father and to "deepen the understanding of what it is to be a family."[6]

Being Realistic about Expectations

The realities of succession planning vary from business to business. In my family, Mary and I had long assumed that our children would be involved in the business. Shaken in our mid-40s by the deaths in rapid succession of Mary's father and both of my parents, we began to plan in earnest. We set several conditions under which our children could join the business:

- They first had to graduate from college.

- They had to work at least five years elsewhere and achieve a management role.

- They had to express an interest in joining the business by the age of 30.

Under different circumstances, one or more of our five children might have stepped into management, but our business was unusual. By the time our children reached the age to consider stepping into management, we already had a lot of high-powered employees. The business had grown so large that the prospect of learning how to lead it looked pretty daunting.

Both as individuals and as a group, our children considered whether they wanted to take the path we had laid out. Each of them had unique attitudes and expectations. Ultimately, all of them decided against joining the company. They realized that the next chairman and CEO of Iams would soon be running a $1 billion company—a huge undertaking. They saw how hard top managers had to work and how much they had to travel. Beyond that, each had unique personal reasons, ranging from involvement in raising small children to the pursuit of other personal dreams and plans to a simple lack of interest. It is important for you as the business owner to remember that each of your children has his or her own set of expectations, hopes, and dreams.

Cheri, daughter of the owners of a first-generation retailer, initially thought she had no interest in the business after seeing how hard her parents worked. However, after spending some years pursuing her artistic interests, she returned and tapped her brother, a former engineer, to help her take over the family business. Even the next generation delved in, helping Cheri and her brother by doing deliveries, being holiday helpers, and taking care of other odds and ends.

However, when it came time to think about handing over the reins, the third generation was unequivocal about the fact that they didn't want to take over. As a result, Cheri and her brother sold off the inventory and closed the business. No hard feelings on her part, she says. "I wonder if there is a fear in many children about whether they can be as successful as their parents."

All business owners face succession challenges unique to their own family and to the size and growth stage of the company.

Planning Your Own Future

One of the ultimate leadership tests for the professional manager is figuring out an exit plan that serves the business. It requires honestly assessing your suitability to continue leading the enterprise.

Part of being a professional manager is seeing and taking responsibility for your own limitations. You may reach a point where you are no longer the right person to run the business. Some entrepreneurs worry that this means the business will fail, but that isn't true; it simply means your role needs to change. Just because you own the business doesn't mean you have to run it. Steve, an Aileron client, faced this squarely. He got his company on track through professional management but realized that he didn't really want to be the one running the company. Everyone agreed that it was in the best interests of the company for his son to step into that role, and Steve went back to doing the job that he loved and gave him a great deal of satisfaction.

Many successful entrepreneurs have understood this and stepped aside when their businesses needed a different kind of leader. McDonald's Corporation's founder, Ray Kroc, stopped running day-to-day operations in 1977 and became senior chairman, deferring to Fred Turner, who he said had "always been an operations man at heart." Kroc said that the change meant, "I no longer jump into the fray in administrative sessions and yell and pound the table." After this shift, he carved out a role that he found even more satisfying: "I am the chief guy when it comes to new-product development and real-estate acquisitions. These are areas for which I have always had a special knack. I always enjoyed them most, so work is even more fun for me now than before."[7]

In making this critical decision, it's important that you get advice from your outside board or trusted mentors or consultants. One business owner hired an industrial psychologist to help him assess an executive as a potential president for his company. He was so convinced the recruit was the right person for the job that he disregarded the psychologist's assessment that the executive would be unable to delegate responsibility. The executive did fine until he passed the 100-employee mark. After that, he lost control and couldn't lead, and he was causing so many morale problems that the business owner had to let him go. If you find good advisors, you stand to save a lot of time and money by listening to them.

Although I don't know who said it, a favorite quote of mine is "Courage is what it takes to stand up and speak. Courage is also what it takes to sit down and listen."[8] So it's important to listen to those you've hired to help you make these decisions.

No matter what your succession and exit plans are, no matter if your children want to take over the business, you can't ignore the future. Just as you wouldn't ignore projected trends, profits, or losses, the future is coming, and it's important to plan for all eventualities.

CONCLUSION

During my journey with The Iams Company, I had many generous mentors. When I asked them, "How can I repay you?" each would respond by telling me to do one thing, "Pay it forward." So, I promised that if I became successful, I would pass on to aspiring business owners the knowledge and understanding I gained from applying professional management principles. This book and the ideas shared in it are one way that I am fulfilling that promise.

We've covered a lot of ground, and I hope you are feeling motivated. Perhaps you're thinking, "What do I do now? How do I make all this work for me and my company?" I hope that you are asking those questions and feeling eager to take some next steps to pursue professional management, because at the end of the day, what I really want you to know is, *this stuff really works*. I can't impress that upon you enough.

If you are willing to do the work and to apply the ideas in this book, you will regain your freedom while regaining control of your business. You will learn how to be successful, profitable, and sustainable by working *on* your business instead of *in* it, by managing results instead of people's activities or behaviors, by stepping back for clarity and perspective.

You don't have to take it on all at once. You can start wherever it works for you in one or two areas that are real problems, where you are ready to try to do things differently. Perhaps that will be in setting direction—articulating your vision and strategic goals—or by installing structure to guide decision making and establishing performance standards to empower more people and to help them be successful. Professional management is a process and a journey, and it will evolve over time throughout all areas of your company. Every step you take will be felt in a meaningful way. Because it is an integrated system, when you make a change and experience a shift in one area, you will feel it in another. You will see results, and that will encourage you. As your employees see results, they will rally behind the changes and urge you on, because they want to be successful, too. Everybody wins.

So, what now?

I hope that you will take steps to learn and live professional management so that you can unleash the potential of your organization, pass on the learning to others, and improve the quality of life for all.

NOTES

Chapter 3: How You Lead

1. Stephen Thomas, "H-E-B president, store worker in Atascocita swap jobs," *YourHoustonNews*, August 6, 2011, www.yourhoustonnews.com/lake_houston/news/article_b873f101-10b3-5eeb-8ee6-d9d9b7833d1f.html (accessed January 13, 2013).

2. Donna Fenn, *Alpha Dogs: How Your Small Business Can Become a Leader of the Pack* (New York: HarperCollins Publishers, 2005), 38–39.

3. Adam Bryant, "What's the Mission?" *New York Times*, March 27, 2011, www.nytimes.com/2011/03/27/business/27corner.html.

4. Kasey Wehrum, "Learning, and Relearning, to Listen," *Inc.* 33, issue 2 (March 2011): 64–68.

5. Peter Drucker, *The Essential Drucker* (New York: Harper-Collins Publishers, 2001), 254–9.

Chapter 4: Your Dream with a Plan

1. Claire Cain Miller and Julie Bosman, "E-Books Outsell Print Books at Amazon," *New York Times*, May 19, 2011, www.nytimes.com/2011/05/20/technology/20amazon.html?_r=0 (accessed January 13, 2013).

2. Claudine Beaumont, "Bill Gates's dream: A computer in every home," *Telegraph*, June 27, 2008, www.telegraph.co.uk/technology/3357701/Bill-Gatess-dream-A-computer-in-every-home.html (accessed January 15, 2013).

Chapter 6: Aligning Your Business with Your Vision

1. Business Model Canvas, www.businessmodelgeneration.com/canvas.

Chapter 7: The Keys to Accountability

1. Helen Coster, "That Was Then: Outdoor Clothier Nau Was Nearly a Victim of Its Own Grand Vision," *Forbes* (March 1, 2010): 54.

2. Michelle A. Barton and Kathleen M. Sutcliffe, "Learning to Stop Momentum," *MIT Sloan Management Review* 51, no. 3 (Spring 2010): 71–76.

Chapter 8: Culture—the Engine Moving Your Business

1. Leigh Buchanan, "Welcome aboard! Now, run!" *Inc.* (March 2010): 95–96.

2. Fenn, *Alpha Dogs*, 84–103.

Chapter 11: Sustainability and Succession

1. Leon Danco, *Beyond Survival* (Edmonton, Alberta, Canada: The Business Family Centre, 2003), 5.

2. Peter Drucker, "Drucker on Management: How to Save the Family Business," *Wall Street Journal* (August 19, 1994), http://online.wsj.com/article/SB10001424052748704204304574544260451524596.html. Ret. November 19, 2009.

3. Meg Cadoux Hirshberg, "Passing the Reins," *Inc.* (March 2011): 37–38.

4. John Ward, *Keeping the Family Business Healthy: How to Plan for Continuing Growth, Profitability, and Family Leadership* (New York: Palgrave Macmillan, 2010), 137–71.

5. Len Costa, "Reviving Horatio Alger," *Forbes* (March 14, 2011): 53.

6. Hirshberg, "Passing the Reins," 37.

7. Ray Kroc, *Grinding It Out: The Making of McDonald's* (New York: St. Martin's Paperbacks, 1987), 166.

8. Although this quote has been widely attributed to Winston Churchill on the Web, Richard Langworth, editor of a scholarly journal published by the Churchill Center in London, has confirmed that it is not an actual Winston Churchill quote. It is what he calls "Churchillian drift."

SELECTED BIBLIOGRAPHY

Barton, Michelle A., and Kathleen M. Sutcliffe. "Learning to Stop Momentum." *MIT Sloan Management Review* 51, no. 3 (Spring 2010): 69–76.

Collins, Jim. *Good to Great: Why Some Companies Make the Leap . . . and Others Don't*. New York: Harper Business, 2001.

Danco, Leon. *Beyond Survival: A Guide for Business Owners and Their Families*. Edmonton, Alberta, Canada: The Business Family Centre, 2003.

Drucker, Peter. *The Essential Drucker: The Best of Sixty Years of Peter Drucker's Writings on Management*. New York: HarperCollins Publishers, 2001.

———. *Innovation and Entrepreneurship*. New York: Collins Business, 1996.

Garfield, Charles. *Peak Performers: The New Heroes of American Business*. New York: William Morrow and Company Inc., 1986.

Ohmae, Kenichi. *The Mind of the Strategist: The Art of Japanese Business*. New York: McGraw-Hill, 1991.

Peters, Thomas J., and Robert H. Waterman Jr. *In Search of Excellence: Lessons from America's Best-Run Companies*. New York: HarperBusiness Essentials, 2004.

Tzu, Sun. *The Art of War*. Center Pillar Publishing, 2010.

Walton, Mary, with W. Edwards Deming. *The Deming Management Method*. New York: Perigee Books, 1986.

Ward, John L. *Creating Effective Boards for Private Enterprises: Meeting the Challenges of Continuity and Competition*. San Francisco: Jossey-Bass Publishers, 1991.

ACKNOWLEDGMENTS

I've learned that writing and publishing a book requires strategic thinking and planning, passion and commitment, and an army of people providing personal and professional support. This book is the result of considerable contributions by many people.

First, I want to thank my wife, Mary, and our children. I deeply appreciate your insights and stories, especially for the chapter on family.

Second, I am grateful to the Aileron staff and supporters, and the private-business owners and thought leaders, who have influenced me. All of you inspire me continually, and you play an important part in perpetuating the learning and sharing of professional management. By doing so, you raise the quality of life for all in your spheres of influence. Thank you to those who generously shared your stories, experiences, and wisdom to inspire and help other business owners to achieve success and enjoyment in owning and running a business. I know this is one of the ways that you have chosen to pay it forward.

Thanks to Steve Piersanti and the entire Berrett-Koehler Publishers team for your belief in this book and in Aileron's values-based professional management system. With your mission, "Creating a world that works for all," and your stewardship model, Aileron and I feel right at home.

Thank you to writer Sue Shellenbarger and developmental editor Margie Adler for your contributions and expertise in shaping the manuscript into a valuable tool for helping private businesses to thrive.

INDEX

ABOUT THE AUTHOR

Clay Mathile understands the challenges of private-business owners. As the former owner of Iams, a company committed to helping dogs and cats to live long, healthy lives through superior nutrition, he increased sales from $12.5 million to $1 billion. Clay cites professional management as one of the critical keys for this growth. In 1999, the Mathile family sold Iams to international conglomerate Procter & Gamble for $2.3 billion.

During his incredibly challenging journey, Clay developed a belief in free enterprise for the greater good. It became a dream for him to help private businesses to become successful, profitable, and sustainable so that they could provide employment in their communities and help their communities to thrive, and in so doing help the people in those communities to have better lives. To turn his passions into a reality, he founded Aileron, a nonprofit foundation. He maintains a tremendous respect for business owners who risk their capital to employ others.

Still active in several business ventures, Clay devotes most of his time to philanthropic interests. In addition to serving as chairman of the board of Aileron, Clay, with his wife, Mary, created the following initiatives to foster hope and inspire change in the Dayton, Ohio, region and around the world:

- The Mathile Family Foundation, which since 1989 has granted more than $230 million to nonprofit organizations that help children and families in need.

- The Glen at St. Joseph, a life-changing campus for 36 single mothers and their young children that is the realization of a longtime dream of Mary's. The Glen offers mothers the opportunity to pursue their educational and career goals while their children attend a state-of-the-art early-learning center on campus.

- The Mathile Institute for the Advancement of Human Nutrition, whose charter is to tackle issues of world hunger and malnutrition. Its mission is to create innovative, effective, and sustainable solutions to alleviate nutritional inadequacies in children.

Clay also serves as a trustee on a select group of nonprofit boards focused on education, medical innovation, and social justice. Clay and Mary live in Dayton, Ohio. Clay insists that his most important roles are husband, father of 5, and grandfather of 15. Life as a family man has led to yet another dream, "a family united forever."

ABOUT AILERON

Aileron is a nonprofit organization established by Clay Mathile to fulfill his commitment to help private businesses grow and to become profitable and sustainable. Since 1996, Aileron has been dedicated to helping private businesses employ proven business practices that can raise the overall effectiveness of their organizations so that they can reach their fullest potential. Aileron has been built upon a foundational belief in free enterprise for the greater good, as well as a dream to help private business.

Aileron is located in Dayton, Ohio. The building and the surrounding campus were designed to be a place for inspiration and reflection as well as a center to foster learning and sharing. The 70,000-square-foot campus sits on 114 mostly wooded acres. Here, business owners can experience courses and workshops where they can learn how to implement professional management. They can work with business advisors or mentors to get individualized support, and they can bring their teams to plan, learn, or work "on" their business. Working with Aileron, clients find clarity and focus on how to make their business better. Everything Aileron offers is to help private businesses grow.

Aileron's Professional Management System is continually evolving, incorporating "what works" and is practical in private business. Aileron lives and studies professional management in private business every day and is made up of experienced business owners who facilitate courses and workshops and provide individualized support to clients. Aileron's commitment and client-centric approach unleashes the potential of private businesses through professional management. Not merely a way to run a business, Aileron's Professional Management is a way of life.

Today, Aileron's clients are growing successful, sustainable businesses. Their businesses are valued resources in their communities, raising the quality of life for many by employing people, supporting families, and, ultimately, building the economy of the country. They are defining their own legacies.